The Book Musical

CROCODILES REMEMBER

by Subash Kundanmal

Inspired By The Memoirs Of
Seth Naomal Hotchand, C.S.I.

Printed in the United States of America

ISBN: 978-1-0880-0166-0

10 9 8 7 6 5 4 3 2 1

A TRIBUTE
By Subash Kundanmal

TO
SETH NAOMAL HOTCHAND, C.S.I.

"Then out spake brave Horatius,
The Captain of the Gate:
To every man upon this earth
Death cometh soon or late.
And how can man die better
Than facing fearful odds,
For the ashes of his fathers,
And the temples of his gods?"

FROM THE POEM 'HORATIUS'

BY LORD THOMAS BABINGTON MACUALAY
1800 - 1859

A BOOKMAKER PROJECT

A SUBSIDIARY of SNEL INC.

Other Works By
Subash Kundanmal

A Song Of Light
Shorts & Briefs
The Plunging Of The Knife
Screenshots

DEDICATED TO

Rao Bahadur Alumal Trikamdas Bhojwani, B.A.

Inspector of Education – Sindh, British India,

and

Sir H. Evan M. James, K.C.I. E., C.S.I.

Commissioner of Sindh, British India

Their collaboration and painstaking efforts breathed life into the Memoirs of Seth Naomal Hotchand, C.S.I., bequeathing soul, sinew and substance to a forgotten chapter of Indian History.

A staged reading of Crocodiles Remember was presented before a live audience at the Edison Theater, University of California, Los Angeles on July 25th 1999.

THE CAST

In order of appearance

Meher Tatna	Narrator
Gagan Sidhu	Narrator
Naveen Kanal	Seth Naomal
Soan Kundanmal	Alu
Shelly Desai	Babaji
Ossie Mair	Seth Hotchand
Robert Broughton	Dr. Burnes
Robert Weir	Col. Henry Pottinger
Maulik Pancholi	Court Jester & Bagree
Ken Kanal	Gulam Ali

THE CAST (Continued)

David Paul Francis	Murad Ali
Sanjay Pandya	Nur Mohammed
Tulsiram Touzene	Ali Akbar
Kiki Thiara	Begum Mumtaz
Sabrinath Touzene	Mohan
Dushyant Bala	Ramji
Andrew Johnson	Seth Hinduja
Hiram Bingham	Capt. Carless

Producers: Naveen Kanal and Jennifer Greer

Director: Kavi Raz

Book: Subash Kundanmal

Music & Lyrics: Subash Kundanmal

Music Arrangement: Craig Fall

Special thanks to

Bindu - Wife, Muse, Inspiration, Companion for numberless grains of sand in the hourglass.

Capt. (Retd.) Mohan Dadlani

Kiki Thiara

Dr. Kishore Mandhyan

Sudha Kishore Punjabi

Meher Tatna

Soan Kundanmal

Bhavna de Montebello

Loretta & Hash Gandhi

Francesca Maria

Empire Publishing & Literary Service Bureau

Harvard University Library

U.S.C. - Marshall School of Business

The Edison Theater

USC - Thornton School of Music

The Cast & Crew of the Staged Reading of Crocodiles Remember

Table of Contents

PROLOGUE

When a chosen few of our folk heroes were taking their final bows on the transient centerstage and the thunderous applause was still in progress, a clique of passionate devotees slipped out of the playhouse to etch golden nimbi around their images. To those honored exemplars of yore who long departed the proscenium arch, we reverently offer our mummeries in especially demarcated hallowed chambers. We pin our earnest hopes on those dearly beloveds in exchange for their benedictions as we yearn for that glorious day when they will perchance grace us with an encore performance.

While we may not be quite as extravagant when the incandescent glare of the spotlights fade and the floodlights go dark on some of our lesser folk heroes, fashioned as they are from the fragile threads of our coarse, common cloth, we nevertheless routinely commemorate their remembrances with exuberant ceremony and generous accolades on days specifically assigned. At our core, it seems we are unabashedly enthralled by folk heroes of every stamp and stripe who stormed the amphitheaters of history's many yesterdays.

It matters little or not at all if many among that venerated species were outright villains, notorious frauds or overrated buffoons, who conceivably deserved to be chased off the footlights, as they dodged the proverbial rotten eggs of scorn lobbed at them by jeering groundlings, even as caustic critics joined in the melee with poison pens of pillory. Perhaps our subliminal yearning for the Shangri-La of everlasting life motivates us to immortalize folk heroes of every ilk who populate our countless chronicles.

Regardless, very few would disagree that each folk hero in his or her onliest fashion contributed to the narrative of our blustering, blundering, creep and crawl from the primordial ooze towards human evolution. While they may occupy but a fleeting residence in our capricious human hearts, they bask in a hazy glow in the antechambers of our collective consciousness with saints and prophets, kings and queens, statesmen and soldiers, conquerors and revolutionaries, writers and artists, discoverers and explorers, inventors and thinkers, and - yes even scoundrels and scallywags.

In Henry IV Part 2, the Earl of Warwick reminds us that "there is a history in all men's lives." The toll of that Shakespearean sagacity rang out loud and clear, not unlike the nineteen chimes of St. Patrick's Cathedral during a winter holiday in New York City, some years before. That Christmas morning, I had finished yet another reading of the Memoirs of Seth Naomal Hotchand. As in prior incursions of that monumental tome, I was quick to spot the warp and waft of history unmistakably braided into the fabric of Seth Naomal's life. This was particularly remarkable since it would be implausible to envision a soothsayer gazing into a crystal ball prophesying Seth Naomal's rendezvous with world history, much less predicting his ascension to the stature of a folk hero.

Seth Naomal could make no claim of illustrious birth, however loosely defined, nor was there a hint or hue of a blue corpuscle coursing through his veins. He was no celebrated champion of gory battles. He was certainly not one of those silver-tongued politicos who are so adept at seducing their coterie of patrons and the gullible public with honey-laced promises of everlasting profit and never-ending leisure, nor was he a member of that holier than thou priestly class who religiously rouse the rabble with heavenly bombast or hellfire oratory. He was a quiet living man, a reticent, risk-averse merchant banker engaged in the prosaic vocation of negotiating currency transactions, promissory notes, and bills of exchange related to the purchase and sale of grains and goats, sugar and sheep, camels and cotton bales, among other commodities - as his forefathers had engaged in for several generations.

2

He was the scion of a renowned mercantile family who resided in the port town of Karachi in the kingdom of Sindh, in north-west India in the nineteenth century. Prattlers in the bazaars and knowledgeable elites of those bygone years seemed to be in agreement that Seth Naomal was one of the wealthiest merchants in South Asia, although his prudence, conservative bent of mind, and innate modesty, obliged him to shun all tawdry exhibitions of gratuitous flamboyance. He was a respected member of the disenfranchised and tyrannized minority Hindu community. Notwithstanding, he and his family were reputed to have unfettered access to luminaries in the highest political echelons in a predominantly Muslim power structure prevalent in the kingdom of Sindh of his day. Yet, it would require precious little to safely surmise that one hundred and fifty years after his passing, his memory might surface upon the discovery of a faded photograph in a family album, lost in an attic of one of his unsuspecting descendants.

To be sure, he had lived a fascinating life during an extraordinary epoch. This ipso facto met the initial smell test of a plethora of tantalizing creative opportunities. Yet upon further reflection, it became clear that additional terra firma required meticulous excavation in order to stake a claim for Seth Naomal as a person of interest so expressly unique as to overcome the hump of a playwright's ingrained inertia. Thus, an exhumation of the historical record, scattered ubiquitously within the pages of literary works of many of his contemporaries, became incumbent and inevitable. Some of those celebrated writers of many yesteryears were well acquainted with his exploits and reputation. In addition, there were accounts of numerous others personally interconnected with his life, many of whom had closely collaborated with him. In time, recognizable sui generis strands interwoven into the design and pattern of Seth Naomal's story began to emerge. Somewhere along the arc of that investigation, Seth Naomal ceased to be an enigma buried in a footnote of a complicated history. Gradually the portrait of a folk hero magically emerged as in a developing tray in a photographer's darkroom.

I embarked upon the acclivitous expedition of writing the Book Musical 'Crocodiles Remember' with a cautious tread of tentativeness until an afterthought as germane as the Duke of Warwick's timeless truth transfigured into an epiphany. It presented itself in the form of a hypothetical question - to wit: If the events that shaped Seth Naomal's personal life had been different, might history have taken another course? There was much in the unimpeachable disinterment to instigate debate over that plausibly daunting imponderable. More significantly though, during that trek of discovery, a motherlode of dramatic material was unearthed with which one could conceivably meld and mold theatrical edifices, personalities, and discourses. That above all else, in my judgment, more than middlingly merited the drudgery of a playwright's labors.

In the nineteenth century, when the sun blazed it's brightest upon the British Empire, and the dominion of India was its crowning achievement, arguably the single most powerful personage on the planet, Her Gracious Majesty Queen Victoria honored Seth Naomal with a letter and an ornate jeweled insignia in a kimkhab pouch. At a grand ceremony held in Karachi, Sindh, on January 1st, 1868, both were presented to him by the British Governor of Bombay, Sir Bartle Frere, who had collaborated with Seth Naomal for many tumultuous years.

The letter read – "VICTORIA, by the Grace of God, of the United Kingdom of Great Britain and Ireland, Queen, Defender of the Faith and Sovereign of the Most Exalted Order of the Star of India, to Seth Naomal of Karachi, greetings: Whereas We being desirous of conferring upon you such a mark of Our Royal Favor as will evince the esteem in which We hold your person and the services which you have rendered to our Indian Empire, We have thought fit to nominate and appoint you to be a Companion of Our Most Exalted Order of the Star of India. We do therefore by these presents grant unto you the dignity of a Companion of the Most Exalted Order of the Star of India and hereby authorize you to have, hold and enjoy the said dignity and rank of a Companion of the Most Exalted Order of the Star of India, together with all and singular, the privileges thereunto belonging and appertaining.

Given at our Court at Osborne House under Our Sign Manual and the Seal of Our Said Order this thirtieth day of April 1866, in the twenty-ninth year of Our Reign.

By Her Majesty's Command (Signed) De Grey and Rippon."

Shortly before Sir Henry Pottinger was appointed the first British Governor of Hong Kong, he was a commissioned officer with the rank of Colonel stationed with the British Army in Colonial India. In that capacity, he was dispatched as a special envoy for the East India Company to the kingdom of Sindh. He worked closely with Seth Naomal and reportedly shared a few hair-raising close calls with him. He wrote to Rear-Admiral Sir Frederick Maitland, British Naval Commander-In-Chief on the eve of the British conquest of Sindh by General Sir Charles Napier, on 28th January 1839: "There is one point to which I solicit your kind and minute attention. I allude to the protection, under all circumstances, of the house, family and property of Seth Naomal of Karachi. That individual is now with this force. He has most zealously and indefatigably assisted us, and I cannot convey my deep anxiety regarding him and his better than by saying that they ought to be guarded as those of the Governor- General of India."

In an essay published in the prestigious Asiatic Quarterly Review in April 1888, Sir Frederic Goldsmid, who had worked extensively with Seth Naomal, wrote: "One alone, whose familiar figure has for years passed away from the midst of his countrymen, may be mentioned by name, the banker Seth Naomal. Connected with what may be called the Intelligence Department of the province of Sindh from the first hour of British occupation, he remained until the period of his demise, the most trustworthy informant and advisor of the several officers who administered the affairs of Sindh. Especially from Baluchistan were his reports of value, for his agents in that quarter had means of ascertaining the state of local politics which even money might not always command. He had a high opinion of European statesmen and would speak of European politics with a significant smile as though he saw through the hidden aims of empires and kingdoms and could unravel tangled skeins which perplex the most learned politicians in the West. His memory is especially noted here, for Karachi (Sindh) in its zenith was not Karachi (Sindh) without Seth Naomal."

"The tangled skeins" and "the hidden aims of empires and kingdoms" that Sir Frederic Goldsmid alluded to in his magnanimous tribute to Seth Naomal was performed on the world stage for the better part of the nineteenth century. The Nobel laureate Rudyard Kipling captured its essence in his celebrated novel, 'Kim'. He popularized the term 'the Great Game' to describe it. It pertained to the clandestine capers during which cadres of rival agents enacted a tournament of shadows, much like performing marionettes, whose strings were attached to the waistbands of two dominant empires of that era, namely Czarist Russia and Imperial Britain. In a monumental contest that spanned a century, their surrogates tirelessly devised elaborate schemes of political and military chicanery to satiate gluttonous cravings for subservient colonies by both those superpowers. In the wake of that marathon competition for dominance, sovereign kingdoms of Asia mutated into groveling protectorates and impotent vassal states.

In 1820, murmurs on the treacherous trails of the Khyber Pass and the Bolan Pass led to a chorus of whispered rumblings by Afghani horse traders, Persian carpet merchants, and Baluchi camel herders who routinely exchanged tidbits of the latest goings-on as they mingled in the crowded tea stalls and the shady opium dens of the local bazaars. The medley of tittle-tattle brought by travelers returning from the Capitals of the Khanates of Central Asia ascended to a crescendo. It resonated in the ears of eavesdropping

British agents, who, in turn, sent disconcerting dispatches that reached the Court of Directors of the East India Company, causing them to refresh their brandies, sit up and take notice.

The crux of the communiques they received suggested in the strongest possible terms that Russia, having accomplished the conquest of Turkistan (Turkey), was stealthily in the thick of an impending military campaign to overrun Afghanistan. British policymakers in London and Calcutta interpreted these ominous intelligence reports to extrapolate that Russia's ulterior intent was to use Afghanistan as a launchpad to challenge British commercial interests and military supremacy in South Asia, which they feared put Great Britain's Indian possessions - 'the jewel in the crown' in imminent jeopardy.

It was not lost on British administrators that it was from the very same mountain passes of Afghanistan that hordes of marauders in the past had invaded India, while the 'unhappy valley' of Sindh had served as the tormented vestibule wherefrom those foreign armies had marched southwards to conquer India's native kingdoms to establish the Moghul Empire. By rare unanimity, both sudden and swift, the independent kingdom of Sindh's proximity to Afghanistan assumed critical significance for British military strategists. Up until this point, except for sporadic commercial contacts with Seth Naomal's business houses for some years prior, the Kingdom of Sindh had been virtually overlooked by the English East India Company, preoccupied, as it was, with the task of consolidating the paramountcy of its commercial and military preeminence in the rest of India.

Never ones to hem and haw when the slow trot of Push threatened to accelerate into a galloping Shove, emissaries of the East India Company commenced diplomatic overtures and treaty-signing expeditions at the Palace of His Majesty Murad Ali Talpur, the Monarch of Sindh. That doddering Regent encumbered by dissensions in his own court, and distracted by violent communal disturbances in his kingdom, helplessly dithered and dodged about, but eventually acquiesced to the stationing of British forces in Sindh to facilitate initiatives to counter Russian ambitions in Afghanistan. The mandatory requirement to cough up an annual contribution to maintain those British troops stationed in his kingdom only added to His Majesty's futile chagrin. Assurances by the envoys of the Honorable East India Company that the noble endeavor of their proposed treaties was to protect the kingdom of Sindh and the company's interests from their common adversaries failed to convince or console him.

To be clear, this erosion of sovereignty of the kingdom of Sindh did not sit well with the Muslim nobles at King Murad Ali's Court. It was also vehemently resented by most members of the royal family who were of the view that advanced age and pleasurable excesses had blunted Mir Murad Ali's sword. Consequently, ominous directives mandated by the hardliners emanated from the cloistered innards of King Murad Ali's palace. The strictures issued threatened dire consequences to the general citizenry of the kingdom of Sindh to discourage them from offering any aid and comfort to the English 'intruders'. The dragline and radial threads of political intrigue and civil discord that followed effectively enmeshed the local citizenry, and Seth Naomal's family in particular, in a web of conflicting loyalties.

In the ensuing communal tensions in the desert kingdom of Sindh, a heinous act of contumely and bigotry revolted the mild-mannered pacifist, Seth Naomal. It transformed him into a committed recalcitrant and a confederate of the East India Company. From there on, his blood was up, and his casus belli became the overthrow of the sixty-year reign of the Talpur rulers of Sindh. It also catapulted him to the stature of an icon of folk history.

It should come as no surprise to the reader that he is primus inter pares among the dramatis personae that inhabit the book musical, 'Crocodiles Remember.' Many of the characters who share the stage with Seth Naomal did exist, although some names have been changed to accommodate a minor technical consideration. For the most part, the events in this work did occur, while other episodes are rearranged and reconstructed for which poetic license is herewith invoked. Obbligato factuality has been synthesized with the ad libitum of fictionality to add tint and texture to augment dramatic heft. No effort has been employed to be slavish to historical hegemony, and those who seek chronological correctness and anecdotal purity are encouraged to dive in and backstroke in the presently placid waters of that bygone era.

In the final analysis, 'Crocodiles Remember' is a creative offering for the diversion of those who wish to spend an hour or two away from their concerns. The 3-time Pulitzer Prize winner, the late great Edward Albee once wrote, "We must never forget that plays are literature and exist as complete experiences on the page. They are not made complete experiences in performance. That is merely an added virtue that a play has." Nonetheless, 'Crocodiles Remember' is designed to be performed on stage by thespians, with the aid and abetment of other creators of illusions who ply those allied arts and crafts that are no less worthy progenies of Mother Theatre.

In this creative offering, no special preference has been allocated to any ideation or dogma over any other. Nor is it a condonement or condemnation of the state of mind of any of the characters. Thus, no mea culpa for their acts and utterances is proffered. Also, this work is not an exercise in polemics, although I suspect that there may be those who will opine otherwise. I am mindful, however, that despite these muscular disclaimers, there are some whose sensibilities will be offended. There may be yet others who will complain that this creative enterprise does not sufficiently validate their perceptions and prejudices. I humbly but unequivocally declare to all detractors of this work that I am a mere minstrel in search of an audience, and in all good conscience, I respectfully refer all those with grievances to approach the Gods of their druthers.

Subash Kundanmal

DRAMATIS PERSONAE

SETH NAOMAL	HINDU MERCHANT BANKER
ALU	SETH NAOMAL GRANDSON
BABAJI	KEEPER OF THE CROCODILES
KING MURAD ALI	REGENT OF SINDH
DR. JAMES BURNES	BRITISH PHYSICIAN
COL HENRY POTTINGER	BRITISH DIPLOMAT
SETH HOTCHAND	SETH NAOMAL'S FATHER
NUR MOHAMMED	HEIR APPARENT
BEGUM MUMTAZ	MURAD ALI'S DAUGHTER
GULAM HUSSEIN	PRIME MINISTER OF SINDH
THE EUNUCH	COURT JESTER

& SIGNIFICANT OTHERS

ACT I

SCENE 1

ACT I
SCENE 1

It is late at night at Muggerpir, a place of pilgrimage in Sindh, India, sometime in the last quarter of the nineteenth century.

AT RISE: The Stage is dark. Gradually a dull bluish glow illuminates it.

(OffStage)

The chirpings of crickets accompany occasional swishing and splashing sounds that suggest a body of water close by. A dog howls in the distance as the clip-clop of horses and the grumble and groans of carriage wheels become louder. The distinct deep throated double hoots of an Indian Eagle Owl and the rustle of dry leaves announce the arrival of whinnying and snorting horses at the Shrine of Muggerpir.

CARRIAGE DRIVER
(OffStage)

Whoa!! Whoa!!

> *OffStage, the door of a carriage opens and shuts.*
>
> *Enter NAOMAL, (50's) – a handsome man dressed in the native garb of a Hindu. He carries a lantern as he escorts his grandson ALU (10).*

NAOMAL

You must be cold! I shall request Babaji to start a fire.

ALU

(Shivering and hugging NAOMAL)

I'm not cold. I want to see the crocodiles, Grandpa! Are they asleep now? What do they eat? Who feeds them? Where do crocodiles come from? I'm cold – But I can't wait to see them, Grandpa!

NAOMAL

Babaji, whom we have come to see, has lived here for a very long time. He is the caretaker of the crocodiles of Muggerpir. When I was a boy, I used to come here with my father to feed them. The crocodiles are sacred to both the Hindus and the Muslims of Sindh, since the beginning.

ALU

The beginning? You mean the beginning of Time? Is that when the English came to Sindh, Grandpa?

NAOMAL

(Amused)

If you behave and do as you are told, the crocodiles of Muggerpir will not only answer all your questions, they may even tell you wondrous stories.

> *The lantern in NAOMAL'S hand creates a strange effect on stage but reveals nothing.*

ALU

How do they know these stories?

NAOMAL

These are no ordinary crocodiles. They possess the souls of those who loved this land so much that they chose to remain here to record the deeds of kings and commoners alike. No

13

trivial detail has escaped them. Even now they peer into your very soul and know every single thought that runs through your mind.

ALU

Will they tell us a story tonight?

NAOMAL

If they are pleased, they might. It is believed that on certain nights they come out and dance in this open compound. Those lucky ones who have earned their special favor will see them. Others cannot. They reveal to those chosen ones the secrets of the past and sometimes of the future. I once brought an Englishman here.
(Wistfully)
It was the day my father left home. I thought he would never come back. He was a good man. We did many things together.

ALU

Grandpa do they know who you are? What happened to your father? Where are the crocodiles?

NAOMAL

First, we must pay our respects to Babaji.

> *They walk towards a door.*
> *NAOMAL knocks, and the door creaks open.*
> *BABAJI enters.*

NAOMAL

Greetings Babaji.

> *He nudges ALU to touch BABAJI'S feet.*

ALU throws himself at BABAJI'S feet and clings to his legs.

NAOMAL
(To ALU)

No! Not like that!

BABAJI

It's all right Seth Naomal. The boy means well. I see that he is here to carry on a great tradition. This is good.
(To ALU)

What is your name, son?

ALU

My name is Alu, short for Alumal.
(He hugs NAOMAL)

He's my Grandpa. His name is Seth Naomal.

The sounds of splashing water become more pronounced.

BABAJI

I know. I hear the crocodiles stirring. Do you hear them? They have eaten well. We are just in time for their nightly dance in the moonlight.

ALU

Babaji,
(As he looks up at NAOMAL)

I wish to hear his father's story.

BABAJI

They remember that story well. It's my favorite one too.
(He smiles)

15

You must come here regularly to feed them. They will reward you with many stories. They remember all that has happened through the endless cycles of births and deaths. They have seen kingdoms rise and fall, fortunes lost and regained, times of golden harvests and the tribulations of famine. Ah! They grow restless.

The splashing sounds continue.

ALU

Do they know you Babaji?

BABAJI

Yes, and they know you too.

ALU

But I have never seen them before.

BABAJI

Shh! We must be quiet now. Come, let us sit in there by the warm fire.

They walk towards the door

BABAJI
(He raises his right arm skyward)

Oh Heavenly Spirit, if it pleases Thee, tell Alu the story of Seth Naomal's father.

They exit the stage through the door.

The backdrop becomes visible, depicting the silhouette of a cactus, a standing camel and another resting in a landscape of endless dunes of sand. A melody begins. The music gets louder and the lighting brighten as dancing CROCODILES enter with pomp and pageantry.

They dance madly around a polished cubic-shaped rock, symbolic of the Kaaba that is revealed centerstage as the music picks up tempo.

A large blue and silver CROCODILE enters as the light blue CROCODILES sway protectively around him and reverently bow to the cubic rock.

A multicolored CROCODILE enters dancing with effeminate grace.

The music reaches a crescendo. Moments later, the music stops. the CROCODILES become motionless.

Amidst puffs of smoke, the CROCODILES are gone. The lighting on stage returns to its original bluish hue, barely revealing anything.

A softer and gentler strain of the music begins to play.

FADE TO BLACK

END OF ACT I
SCENE 1

ACT I

SCENE 2

ACT I
SCENE 2

SETTING: *The Royal Durbar, (Audience Hall,) of KING MURAD ALI, Regent of Sindh, in his palace at Hyderabad, Sindh in the 1830's.*

The set reflects the opulence of an oriental king's court. The Stage is adorned with midget palm trees in gilded planters. A large painting depicts an image of the cubic rock and a blue and silver crocodile being worshipped by several crocodiles. Close to the painting is a window that is partially open. Delicate white woodwork supports some light shrubbery to suggest that the window overlooks the palace gardens. Upstage sits a magnificent screen depicting gilded carvings of fish and seabirds. It has small cutouts. It permits no view of what lies behind it. The other dominant piece of furniture in the room is a majestic silver throne cushioned in blue, silver and gold. A cushioned silver footrest lies in front of it. By the side of the throne is a carved ivory table on which is placed a silver tray, a wine decanter and goblets. Close to the throne is a silver bowl that serves as the royal spittoon.

The strain of the same music continues softly from the previous scene.

The lighting on stage suggests a bright desert evening.

ATTENDANTS dressed in light blue shirts and loose trousers, (salwars and khameezes) wait on the GUESTS at the royal reception.

The GUESTS engage in polite inaudible conversations as they greet each other.

The costumes worn by the GUESTS exhibit the diversity of India during that period. Muslim noblemen in tall hats and ornate robes co-mingle. A Parsi in his ceremonial jammeh and sarband appears to be in conversation with a high-ranking Officer of Sindh's Imperial Army, dressed in formal military attire. There are two Englishmen present. DR. JAMES BURNES (40), a red-faced middle-aged man in a serious black suit. His companion is COL. HENRY POTTINGER (30), the British envoy in Sindh. He is a handsome British officer dressed in a red military coat decorated with medals.

The Englishmen are in earnest conversation with two Indians. The older Indian is SETH HOTCHAND, (50's), a Hindu Merchant-Banker. He is elegantly dressed in a long jacket and pants to match. He wears a turban in the style of an upper-class Hindu of that period. On his forehead he has a red mark --a 'tilak', traditionally worn by high caste Hindus. The younger Indian is his son, SETH NAOMAL, (mid 20's), a younger version of the older man in the first scene. His face is fresh and youthful. He is elegantly dressed in a matching suit and turban.

Women are conspicuous by their absence.

HOTCHAND
(As he surveys the room)
This Durbar Hall has not changed over the years.

NAOMAL
(Drily)
Like everything else in Sindh.

BURNES
Personally, I like this Durbar Hall. Royal receptions, banquets and always such great entertainment! Oh, how I love a good party!

(To POTTINGER)

I'm looking forward to this one. It's a yearly affair King Murad Ali hosts. One never knows what to expect.

POTTINGER

Bah! Parties, receptions, banquets, durbars! I thought the pomp and fuss at Calcutta was bad enough. I wonder how anything ever gets accomplished in this damnable desert. I have been here for over a month and nothing has been done.

BURNES

Thank the Lord it's getting a little cooler though, isn't it?

POTTINGER

Small mercies!

(To NAOMAL, good humoredly)

I say Naomal, do you suppose we could chat with His Majesty sometime this year?

NAOMAL

(He smiles and looks furtively around)

I think there may be opportunity tonight. Our people succeeded in making contact with Gulam Ali, the Prime Minister. These things take time Henry. Besides it's much too dangerous for Hindus to show too much influence at His Majesty's Court. The Muslims of Sindh resent us enough already. It only creates more trouble.

HOTCHAND

(Scanning the room cautiously)

God knows there has been enough lately.

POTTINGER

What sort of trouble?

NAOMAL

(Continues to look furtively around)

The usual. The nobility in Sindh hunt animals in their private forests, while the Muslims in the bazaars of Sindh hunt the Hindus. You know, beat up a Hindu shopkeeper, rape a Hindu woman, kidnap a Hindu child. It's been going on for years and has only been getting worse. Of late the Hindus have been fighting back. Dr. Burnes can tell you. He has been in Sindh for some time now.

BURNES

I have hardly gotten around that much. I have been mostly at the palace, attending to His Majesty. As you know his left eye was badly infected. It's much better now, of course.

(To HOTCHAND)

But you haven't done so badly yourselves, being Hindus, I mean. Your businesses flourish, you trade all over India and abroad. I've seen you both often enough at the Palace. You are here at all the parties and receptions. Things can't be all that bad now, can they? Let's just enjoy ourselves, shall we?

> NAOMAL is about to respond, but
> HOTCHAND gives him a discouraging look.

BURNES

I hope Nur Mohammed is not going to be here tonight to spoil the fun!

(Unconsciously his voice becomes louder)

He has this abominable habit of glaring at people with suspicion. Gets rather uncomfortable when he's around.

22

POTTINGER, NAOMAL and HOTCHAND look around, smile and nod at the other guests who have noticed them.

POTTINGER
(Anxiously)
Who the devil is he?

NAOMAL
The devil himself!

HOTCHAND
(He draws the group closer)
They call him the Ogre of Sindh. Hindus and Muslims alike fear him, as children shudder in the darkness of the desert nights.

HOTCHAND slowly walks away from the screen positioned at stage left. He invites the group to join him there.

HOTCHAND
(He eyes the screen)
Prince Nur Mohammed is heir apparent to the throne. He is married to His Majesty's daughter, Begum Mumtaz. She usually sits behind that screen accompanied by her lackeys when King Murad Ali holds court. She watches all that transpires.

NAOMAL
King Murad Ali takes little interest in his sons. but he adores Begum Mumtaz. She's the favorite of the Talpur Clan and is the proverbial 'power behind the throne.'

BURNES

And that damn Nur Mohammed is the power behind the power behind the throne.

HOTCHAND

He is determined to be the next ruler of Sindh. It is well known that Begum Mumtaz and her people at Court want that very much.

POTTINGER

Is he the fellow who has arranged our meeting with His Majesty this evening?

NAOMAL

Dear God, No! It was Prince Gulam Ali, His Majesty's cousin who serves as his Prime Minister. Begum Mumtaz and Nur Mohammed detest him. But he is an able and fair administrator. If it wasn't for him there would be no Hindus left in Sindh.

BURNES

Nor any Englishmen for that matter.

> *Trumpets blast cheerfully, followed by the boom of drums as the music begins. All on stage find their places as attendants and guards stand at attention.*
>
> *A court ATTENDANT dressed in a light blue uniform, (salwar & kameez) enters walking backwards. He has a large fan of peacock feathers in his hand and is fanning KING MURAD ALI (50's) as he enters. MURAD ALI is flanked by two impressive looking men. The younger of the two is PRINCE NUR MOHAMMED, 30, the heir apparent to the throne. He is perfectly attired in a sherwani*

and wears a sword sheathed in a gilded scabbard. He is diabolically handsome with a well-trimmed beard and mustache. His flashing eyes survey the GUESTS.

The other is GULAM ALI, (60), Prime Minister, cousin and confidante of KING MURAD ALI. He is also attired in an elegant sherwani. He is possessed of a mature serenity and an air of dignity. He has a graying beard and a kindly face.

MURAD ALI waddles up to the throne without ceremony.

COURTIERS and ATTENDANTS shower him with flower petals.

THE GUESTS bow deeply.

MURAD ALI nods back in acknowledgment.

The music stops abruptly. There is a momentary hush. MURAD ALI eyes the spittoon on the floor. He bends forward and lets out a steady stream of red spittle. It barely makes it in the silver spittoon. He grins at his guests, exposing red-stained teeth. He chews a concoction of tobacco, opium and betel-nuts. The guests give him a rousing ovation. A servant picks up the spittoon, and places another at the same spot.

The music starts to play again.

Enter A JUGGLER juggling short knives.

The GUESTS applaud.

Enter a FIRE EATER blowing gusts of flames.

The GUESTS applaud.

Enter two beautiful scantily clad DANCERS with nearly transparent veils.

The GUESTS applaud.

Enter the COURT JESTER. He is an awkward looking individual. He wears heavy makeup and female attire. He is a hijra (a eunuch), feminine in his gestures and demeanor with the facial structure and the frame of a man. He clowns about mimicking the dancers.

KING MURAD ALI finds the COURT JESTER's vulgar antics hilarious. The GUESTS applaud.

AN ATTENDANT brings the silver wine goblet to MURAD ALI on a tray. MURAD ALI drinks deeply from it and returns it. The ATTENDANT will perform this ritual throughout this scene.

The tenor and tempo of the Music changes as the two DANCERS exit the stage. The COURT JESTER continues to dance, making gestures of adulation to MURAD ALI. He begins to sing the State Anthem of Sindh.

COURT JESTER
(Singing)

BETWEEN THE MOUNTAINS AND THE PLAINS OF HIND,

LIE THE GOLDEN SANDS OF BELOVED SINDH,

ALL SINDHIS HAIL IN A SINGLE VOICE,

MIR MURAD ALI IS ALLAH'S CHOICE.

(All on stage join in repeating the last line).

26

MIR MURAD ALI IS ALLAH'S CHOICE.

COURT JESTER
(Singing)

HIS RULE IS WISE, HIS EDICTS FAIR,

BUT ALL INFIDELS BEWARE,

FOR BELIEVERS HAIL IN A SINGLE VOICE,

MIR MURAD ALI IS ALLAH'S CHOICE.

(Sung by all on stage)

MIR MURAD ALI IS ALLAH'S CHOICE.

(Chorus)

ALLAH ALMIGHTY AND HIS PROPHET PURE,

GAVE MURAD ALI TO SINDH AS THE CURE,

TO RID THE LAND OF THE INFIDEL RACE,

TO FLOWER THE DESERTS WITH ISLAMIC GRACE.

COURT JESTER
(Singing)

MIR MURAD ALI OF TALPUR FAME,

WILL BRING INFIDELS TO THEIR KNEES IN SHAME,

TILL ALL HAIL IN A SINGLE VOICE,

MIR MURAD ALI IS ALLAH'S CHOICE.

(Sung by all on stage)

ALLAH ALMIGHTY AND HIS PROPHET PURE

GAVE MURAD ALI TO SINDH AS THE CURE,

TO RID THE LAND OF THE INFIDEL RACE,

TO FLOWER THE DESERTS WITH ISLAMIC GRACE

(Sung by all the courtiers and some guests on stage with passion)

HAIL MURAD ALI - ALLAH'S CHOICE!

HAIL MURAD ALI – ALLAH'S CHOICE!

HAIL MURAD ALI – ALLAH'S CHOICE!

(End of song)

There is a hush as all eyes turn to MURAD ALI. He gives Prime Minister GULAM ALI a nod. GULAM ALI signals two ATTENDANTS. They approach MURAD ALI with a handsome chest. The COURT JESTER is summoned to approach MIR MURAD ALI.

The COURT JESTER prostrates before MURAD ALI with exaggerated humility and reverence. He grovels at MURAD ALI'S feet. MURAD ALI dips his podgy bejeweled hand into the chest that is filled with an assortment of shiny baubles. He weighs the contents in his hand and showers it over the COURT JESTER's head.

The COURT JESTER howls like a happy dog and prances about on all fours. He sticks his tongue out and pants like an excited canine. He begins a mock chase after the treasure. He pretends to stuff some of the baubles in his ears and under his arms, He showers it over his head and tries to stuff it up his behind. He rolls over on his back and sprinkles it over his chest and belly.

28

He stuffs his mouth with it. He pretends to snarl and chew. He coyly stuffs his bosom with the treasure. He begins to bark again. He moves on all fours around the guests and courtiers, growling and snarling.

He stops at a GUARD who is standing at rigid attention. He sniffs the GUARD'S leg and pretends to lick his ankle. He lifts his own leg and pretends to urinate on the GUARDS leg. The GUARD moves away in mock annoyance and chases him about. The GUARD kicks out at him. The COURT JESTER yelps and howls like a dog in pain, and with the GUARD in pursuit he exits the stage.

All through the COURT JESTER's antics, MURAD ALI shakes with laughter, occasionally wiping his tears. The GUESTS applaud.

A few GUESTS approach the throne. They bow deeply as they are introduced inaudibly to MURAD ALI, alternatively by GULAM ALI and NUR MOHAMMED.

MURAD ALI exchanges a few inaudible words with them giving each a fistful of gaud drawn from the chest as they exit the stage.

At the end of this brief ceremony, MURAD ALI exits with NUR MOHAMMED and the rest of his entourage.

GULAM ALI approaches POTTINGER, BURNES, HOTCHAND and NAOMAL.

GULAM ALI
(Smiling)
Colonel Pottinger, you illuminate this Court by your presence.
(Addressing BURNES)

Dr. Burnes, you of course are always welcome at the Palace. I know His Majesty would be pleased if you made your home here with us.

(Flippantly)

Your medicines work wonders on believers and non-believers alike and you would find no dearth here of either who need your services.

(To POTTINGER)

I do hope you enjoyed the evening's entertainment.

POTTINGER

Excellency, A most pleasurable evening indeed. I have also enjoyed getting to know your fair country, thanks to Dr. Burnes, Seth Hotchand and Seth Naomal. But there is pressing unfinished business that brought me here to Hyderabad. While I have waited to meet with His Majesty, Seth Hotchand and Seth Naomal have urged me not to lose heart. They have the highest regards for you and assure me that His Majesty values your judgment above all others.

HOTCHAND

Highness, Hindus and Muslims alike agree that you are an indispensable advisor to a noble King.

GULAM ALI

(To POTTINGER)

We have been informed of your request, and have had occasion to read the kind letter sent by his Excellency, the Governor General. Allah, as you well know Colonel, is with those who are patient. I have suggested to His Majesty to hear your petition tonight and if Allah permits, matters will be resolved to the satisfaction of all parties.

POTTINGER

We are most obliged to you for arranging this audience with
His Majesty.

GULAM ALI
(To NAOMAL)

I am informed that you travel extensively these days. Do come
and visit me sometime. I am always eager to learn more about
happenings abroad.

NAOMAL

Highness, it would be my honor.

> *All during this exchange COURT ATTENDANTS bring
> in cushioned munjis, (low chairs) that are placed on both
> sides of the throne. The bustle of activity intensifies as more
> ATTENDANTS enter and exit in preparation of a private
> audience with MURAD ALI.*

> *With less fanfare and pomp than in his earlier appearance,
> MURAD ALI enters, accompanied by NUR
> MOHAMMED. MURAD ALI sits on the throne as a
> COURT ATTENDANT hands him a goblet.*

GULAM ALI

I must attend to His Majesty. He tires easily these days.

> *He walks towards the throne. KING MURAD ALI smiles
> at the waiting group. He invites them to sit down. They
> bow and take their seats.*

MURAD ALI
(To POTTINGER)

My dear Cousin Gulam Ali tells me it is time for us to order some English furniture for our Durbar Hall. We have this feeling that we will be seeing more of you and your countrymen in the days to come.

He laughs heartily.

POTTINGER
(Smiling)
Your Majesty, the Governor General wishes me to inform you that he prays for your continuing good health. Dr. Burnes is satisfied that the infection you suffered poses no further danger to your eye.

MURAD ALI
Praise be to Allah! Dr. Burnes has performed noble service to our blessed self. Do convey our sincere sentiments of goodwill to the Governor General for his kindness in dispatching Dr. Burnes to us. We have invited Dr. Burnes to make his home with us in Sindh, but he speaks of a wife in England. We are surprised to hear he has only one. Why, the good doctor could have several here and surely that would improve his health!

All present smile and laugh politely.

BURNES
Thank you, thank you, Majesty, the one at home is plenty, but I must say my stay here has been most agreeable – never a dull moment.

MURAD ALI
Do stay a while Dr. Burnes. We enjoy your good company and besides who knows my right eye might need you next week!
(To SETH HOTCHAND and SETH NAOMAL)

Welcome my wise and good friends. Your presence at our Court must give much comfort to our Hindu subjects. No doubt they must sing praises in their temples in honor of their benevolent Monarch who permitted them the liberty to worship those stone statues that they call their Gods!

(He laughs good-naturedly)

HOTCHAND
(Smiling)

Sire, we are heartened that our petition to you did not go unheeded. There is relative tranquility in the kingdom due to it.

NUR MOHAMMED
(Curtly)

We hear to the contrary from our sources, Majesty. We are informed that the opening of Hindu temples permitted by your edict at the behest of Seth Hotchand and Seth Naomal and their band of unbelievers and idol-worshippers, have become breeding grounds for revolt. The blood of our Muslim brothers has been shed. Hindu shops have closed at least a dozen times causing much inconvenience to the general citizenry.

NAOMAL
(Calmly)

Your Majesty, Hindus in large numbers have been killed and maimed as well. Our women have been raped, our businesses and shops looted and burnt to the ground, our children forced to pledge fidelity to Islam that is averse to our traditions.

MURAD ALI
(Yells)

Enough!

GULAM ALI
(With dignity)

This is not the time to discuss these matters. We must be considerate of our English guests.

MURAD ALI

Yes! Yes! We must be considerate of our English guests.
(To POTTINGER)

Just a little family matter– pay no attention to it. Tell me Colonel what may we do for you?

POTTINGER

In his letter to Your Majesty, the Governor General was pleased to inform you that Seth Hotchand and Seth Naomal have been appointed exclusive commercial agents for the Honorable East India Company in Sindh. I was delegated here to request a waiver of the jizyah, the Hindu tax, imposed upon the goods handled by their firms on our account. It places the Honorable Company in an unfavorable position.

NUR MOHAMMED

The jizyah is proscribed in the Quran, besides it is a source of considerable revenue to our Treasury. We cannot merely waive it. We need to know more. Why do business with the Dhummies, the lower class when there are Muslim firms in Sindh that you could appoint as your agents. Why not choose among them, if you wish to avoid the jizyah?

POTTINGER

For the last ten years the firms of Seth Hotchand and Seth Naomal have traded regularly with the Company throughout India and abroad. Their appointment has been made at the highest levels and is viewed to be in the best interests of the honorable Company.

NAOMAL

Let me add, Your Majesty, that the customs revenue on account of the trade with the company, will be far greater than any loss to the Treasury due to the waiver of the tax.

HOTCHAND

In the neighboring kingdom of Cutch, where no such tax is imposed, our trading contributes to 40,000 gold mohurs each year in custom revenues alone.

GULAM ALI
(Diplomatically)

Colonel, please rest assured that we will give the matter our most serious consideration. A decision will be reached on that question in the next few days.

POTTINGER

Thank you, Excellency. In his letter the Governor General also requested Your Majesty's permission for one of our merchant ships to traverse the river Indus, which flows through your domains. The ship will be transporting Arabian horses that His Majesty, the King of England wishes to present to His Royal Highness, Maharaja Ranjit Singh of the Punjab.

There is a tense silence.

GULAM ALI

The waters at this time of year are dangerous to navigate. No doubt an escort by our commanders to your ship would give your Governor General much comfort.

NUR MOHAMMED
(Sharply)

We are not entirely unaware of the happenings in the countries around us Colonel. Today it is some horses, tomorrow more horses, then soldiers and guns. Then more soldiers and more guns. We do not wish to turn our kingdom into a cross-road of warring foreigners.

POTTINGER

While we are on the subject of the countries around you Sire, the Governor General has received confirmed reports of Russian plans to invade India. As Your Majesty is aware, they have already overrun Turkistan.

NUR MOHAMMED

A few years ago, your Government told us that the French were meditating an attack upon us and we were asked to exclude them from trading in our territories. Now you say the Russians are coming. We also hear that your Government wishes to place that venomous snake Shah Shuja on the throne in Afghanistan so that he may once again harass our border towns and exact tribute from us, as he did in the past.

POTTINGER

It is in the interests of the Kingdom of Sindh and that of the Honorable East India Company to place a strong defense in Afghanistan, for if the Russians ever march into Kabul, they would control the high ground and swoop down on your border town of Shikarpur which sits waiting to be taken. Within a matter of days, Russian troops would move towards your Capital. Even if your forces should succeed in repelling their advances, the Russians will annex all captured territories and hold them to ransom. The Russians have refused to sign all treaties. The time to prepare is now.

NUR MOHAMMED
(Sarcastically)
I hope your Governor General recognizes that Sindh is a sovereign kingdom that stalwartly reserves the right to conduct its own foreign policy and has its own armed forces to protect its interests.

Another tense silence.

GULAM ALI
Majesty, the good Colonel merely explains the concerns of His Excellency, the Governor General on the matter. It is appropriate to give a fair hearing to Colonel Pottinger even if we should not always agree with his assessments.

NUR MOHAMMED glares hatefully at GULAM ALI.

POTTINGER
(Emphatically)
The Sovereignty and the very independence of Sindh is in grave danger, Majesty. Shah Shuja is one of your own Faith and an ally of the British in India. His return to Afghanistan is in our common interests.

NUR MOHAMMED
(Heatedly)
We are prepared to deal with eventualities that threaten our domains in our own way and in our own time.

MURAD ALI
(Raises his arm to stop all further discussions)
However, Colonel, we have every desire to accommodate the King of England, and as a gesture of our continuing goodwill to Maharaja Ranjit Singh of Punjab, we will permit the passage of your Company's ship through our waters.

NUR MOHAMMED
We must insist Sire that under no circumstances should there be any transportation of military stores or troops now or at any time through Sindh. It is further understood that our Commanders will escort the English vessel during its passage through our territorial waters.

POTTINGER
(Evading the remark from NUR MOHAMMED)
Thank you, Your Majesty. May I say how grateful we are for your most valuable time and consideration. There is one additional matter that needs Your Majesty's attention. For several months now we have petitioned your Governor Ahmad Bugree for permission to take soundings at the Port of Karachi. The purpose of these scientific investigations is to determine the condition of the harbor entrance. We believe that this will help safeguard men and material of all merchant ships that trade regularly at the port.

GULAM ALI
Who is to conduct these soundings Colonel?

POTTINGER

Captain Carless, a most qualified officer attached to the Honorable Company's Naval Station in Bombay. He will be assisted by his staff under the supervision of your port authorities, of course.

GULAM ALI

Is this likely to disturb trade at the port?

POTTINGER

To the contrary Excellency. We would be able to dredge sand and debris deposits at the entrance of the harbor for the benefit of all trading ships that enter the port.

NAOMAL

Several ships have been grounded in recent months causing a severe disruption of trade.

MURAD ALI

We see no reason to refuse a request that benefits trade and improves our port facilities.

NUR MOHAMMED

But Majesty...

MURAD ALI
(To GULAM ALI)
Please inform our Governor at Karachi of our decision.

POTTINGER

Thank you, Your Majesty.

MURAD ALI

Go in peace Colonel and convey our salaams to your Governor General.

> *BURNES, POTTINGER, NAOMAL and HOTCHAND rise. All bow deeply. POTTINGER and NUR MOHAMMED eye each other guardedly.*
>
> *GULAM ALI motions HOTCHAND and NAOMAL to stay as the Englishmen are escorted off stage by court officials. MURAD ALI takes a deep gulp from his goblet. He motions to HOTCHAND and NAOMAL to resume their seats.*

MURAD ALI

Indulge us, Seth Hotchand. Let us talk as did our fathers in days gone by. Tell us what is good in our dominions and that which ails our people. You are out there and are able to take the pulse. You witness the happy smile and the angry brow, the satisfied and the sullen look. We are so far removed from it, enshrined within these palace walls, entombed alive. Frankly, we are unable to fathom the cause of this continuing violence in our lands.

(He raises his goblet)

It has caused our spirits to be low of late.

HOTCHAND

It grieves me to hear you say this Majesty. Perhaps a change of air may soothe your heart. The climate at Karachi is so agreeable at this time of year. We could ride and talk away the hours, of poetry and philosophy, and the ways of our ancestors. We did that in the days when we were younger, when our burdens did not weigh us down. I myself am weary of the troubles in our villages and towns. Frankly, Your

40

Majesty, these communal tensions haunt my waking moments and rob me of my sleep.

MURAD ALI

Why these frequent and bitter clashes between the people of Sindh? That question torments my mind. Hotchand, dear friend, why can't they be like us, or is it that the comfort we feel in each other's company blinds us to the real differences between the Hindus and Muslims of Sindh? Perhaps our friendship clouds our understanding of the true state of affairs in our kingdom. These riots in Sindh are becoming daily events. There must be a solution.

NUR MOHAMMED

Should you command, I would have the bones of every idol-worshipping Hindu dog in Sindh reduced to a fine powder and transported to the wastelands of the Thar Desert.

GULAM ALI

With respect...,

NAOMAL

(Calmly)

Hindus living in all parts of Sindh engage in peaceful trade. They are the tillers of the soil, hardworking traders and shopkeepers.

HOTCHAND

(Restrains NAOMAL with a motion of his hand)

Since the days of our ancestors, we have remained steadfast and faithful in our obedience of the kingdom's just laws. Hindus have added to the prosperity of Sindh, and may I add our enterprises have contributed much to the State Treasury. We have...

NUR MOHAMMED

Leave it! Leave it! You make a tidy profit from your enterprises you...you... Hindus! You lend your monies and tie the noose of debt around the necks of our Muslim citizens.

NAOMAL

(Rises from his seat)

We are merchants and bankers and we admit it without shame.

GULAM ALI

Let us be calm!

MURAD ALI

Stop it! Stop it! I cannot bear this bickering any longer!

There is a tense silence. NUR MOHAMMED glares at GULAM ALI.

NUR MOHAMMED

Majesty, if I was not impeded by the hypocritical dogs who defile the Holy Quran and still dare to call themselves Believers – yes Muslims at this court who have fallen prey to the vile intrigues of these infidels, I would cut to pieces all in our kingdom, who will not acknowledge Allah, the Compassionate, the Merciful as the one and only God.

HOTCHAND

Majesty, respectfully may I say, that this is the mentality that sparks riots in Sindh. Sentiments such as these sow seeds of intolerance that incite the illiterate and untutored. It is this attitude, devoid of all reason, that pits Muslim against Hindu, causing us to live in a state of constant warfare in our communities and neighborhoods. Sire, I am now forced to

42

speak from the heart and I beg the favor of your indulgence if what I say causes you discomfort.

(NAOMAL attempts to restrain his father).

MURAD ALI

Dear friend, have you not always spoken freely? Did we not consult you on the tax laws? Certain positions in our Government are held by individuals recommended by you and others of your faith. We have fostered reforms of our laws, permitted the opening of Hindu places of worship, and yet there is this rampant violence over petty incidents.

NAOMAL

The people of Sindh have the greatest respect for you Your Majesty...

HOTCHAND

Sadly, there still exist practices in Sindh that are encouraged by the tacit sanction of the law - acts so unspeakably vile that Hindus in particular, among other minorities, consider death to be preferable.

MURAD ALI

Vile? What are these vile practices in my kingdom that makes death more welcome among your people? I always thought I understood the Hindus in my kingdom because I understood you so well, Hotchand. But today I cannot fathom what it is that you speak of.

GULAM ALI

Perhaps we should discuss this at another time. It has been a long evening, Majesty and you need to rest from the exhausting events of the day.

MURAD ALI

(Signals for more drink)

No! No! We desire to hear this. The ways of the Hindus have always held a strange fascination for me. Their rituals and philosophies are quaint and charming although they are different from our own. Now Hotchand speaks of something they consider worse than death. What could it be? Speak Seth Hotchand.

HOTCHAND

Sire, it may offend you to know.

MURAD ALI

I command you, old friend! Keep us no longer in suspense.

(There is a pregnant silence)

HOTCHAND

There is a practice prevalent in our beloved land and the keepers of law and order in the realm look the other way when it occurs. Yet it is so odious, unjust, and cruel that Hindus in large numbers have fled to the neighboring kingdoms of Cutch and Punjab to escape that dreaded fate.

NUR MOHAMMED

(Angrily)

Go Hindu dogs, leave Sindh! You are not wanted here. This would be a better land without you, for the mosques would resound with the prayer, "Praise be to Allah, Lord of the Creation, The Compassionate, the Merciful, King of Judgement-day! You alone we worship and to You alone we pray for help. Guide us to the straight path, the path of those You have favored, not of those who have incurred Your wrath, nor of those who have gone astray." May those voices in our Mosques be so loud that it is heard all around the world.

MURAD ALI
(Containing his impatience)

We wish no further interruption. Hotchand speak! What is this vile thing that causes the people of your faith to leave their homes and risk misadventures in other lands? I wish to hear this now. I do not want to hear anything else until I know what it is that you speak of.

HOTCHAND

We Hindus are no strangers to suffering, yet Majesty, that which we dread the most is practiced throughout the kingdom with alarming regularity and in broad daylight. Hindus are routinely seized upon for the slightest excuse, forced to disown their own faith to swear allegiance to Islam. Against all norms of decency, they are circumcised in the presence of all! This humiliation is endured by Hindus regardless of their age and station. We view this to be the worst of our calamities.

As HOTCHAND speaks, somber music begins.

Downstage: Enter a turbaned HINDU and his WIFE whose face is covered by a shawl. Two MUSLIMS follow the HINDU and his WIFE. The MUSLIMS knock the HINDU'S turban and attempt to manhandle his WIFE. The angry HINDU attempts to free his WIFE. Another MUSLIM enters the stage and joins in to overpower the HINDU. A shoving match ensues. The HINDU is knocked to the ground and two MUSLIMS, one with a book in his hand, the other wielding a knife, attack the Hindu. The other MUSLIM runs off with the distraught WIFE. The

MUSLIMS bolt off stage. The HINDU lies writhing in pain.

NAOMAL

To those who have suffered this fate, the Sun itself has been blotted out. News of these injustices spread like a fire in the undergrowth, enflaming emotions, raising, fears and suspicions. They speak in hushed whispers in the bazaars of those to whom this has happened.

Downstage: Enter a VENDOR of pots and pans. He passes by the HINDU on the ground. A PASSERBY enters carrying firewood who whispers to an accompanying WOMAN with a basket of vegetables on her head. They huddle around the fallen Hindu. BABAJI in his black robe enters and sits by his side. He raises his arm skyward.

HOTCHAND

And those unfortunate ones are not seen again even by their own kith and kin. For shame they shun the companionship of family, friends and neighbors. They feel they are misfits in any society. They live as outcasts and crawl out at nightfall eating the remains in the bazaars. They call them "People of the Night."

The lights in the foreground change to indicate night. The PEOPLE OF THE NIGHT, in tattered clothes, enter. Some carry candles. They shield their faces with shawls. They walk by the fallen HINDU and lift him up on his feet. They exit the stage in a slow procession. BABAJI follows. He raises his right arm skyward.

NAOMAL

Among the People of the Night are those who were once responsible and respected members of society, sons, husbands, fathers, who pledged their allegiance to Your Majesty and to the Kingdom of Sindh.

The Music stops. NUR MOHAMED seems ready to explode. MURAD ALI takes a large gulp from his goblet.

HOTCHAND

Forgive me Majesty, I can say no more. Just the thought of it causes me to shudder. In the name of all that is sacred and good, I implore you to forbid this abhorrent practice. I fear it will one day set Sindh ablaze, and in that fire all we have worked for together will perish and amount to naught.

NUR MOHAMMED

You dare criticize a commandment of the Holy Quran! It is written that all infidels be given an opportunity to acknowledge Allah as the One and only God. It is the birthright, nay the supreme duty of every true believer to faithfully follow the teachings of the Holy Book. How dare you be so bold as to suggest to His Majesty, appointed by Allah to propagate the Faith. to revoke Quranic Decree! These unbelievers, these bloated merchant princes may have those infidel English dogs under their spell, but they cannot fool me with their pretended fidelity to the kingdom of Sindh, for it is confirmed Majesty, that this very same man, this sanctimonious Hindu hypocrite and his son, encouraged the accursed Hindu merchants to shut their shops just the other night. It sparked an uproar in the town and led to the deaths of two of our brothers in faith.

HOTCHAND

Prince Nur Mohammed, why do you speak of me in this way? Surely you cannot believe that I would act averse to the traditions of my own faith and instigate such brutal acts.

NAOMAL

(Calmly)

Your Majesty, ten Hindus were killed, many more injured, a large number still missing. Our warehouse by the Port in Karachi had been robbed. A chase ensued. A Muslim caught red-handed with the goods in his possession. Tempers rose and people were drawn to the commotion in large numbers. A few Muslims began to beat the manager of the warehouse. Hindu shopkeepers in the area rallied to his support. Within moments shops were set ablaze. My father and I arrived on the scene and summoned the constables. We pleaded with the Hindus to desist from further acts of violence and to go home to their families.

NUR MOHAMMED

Lies! Lies! It was never proved that a Muslim looted the warehouse.

GULAM ALI

We have received a full report of the incident from the Governor of the Province. The lootoo Your Majesty, is one Ali Akbar, who had his ears cut off only last year for another offense. He is now in custody awaiting judgment.

> GULAM ALI *claps his hands. A GUARD bring in ALI AKBAR who appears badly beaten. His arms are tied behind his back. His face is bloated, his clothes dirty. He is*

draped by a cloth that covers his ears. He prostrates before the throne and weeps out a confession.

ALI AKBAR

Mercy Majesty! How unfortunate I am! It was a slow day. There was no baksheesh to be had. Why did I do it? I do not know!

NUR MOHAMMED
(Angrily)

Shut your foul mouth, haramzadah! You took an oath on the Holy Quran just yesterday, that you were only trying to find a place to sleep for the night.

NUR MOHAMMED glares at ALI AKBAR and motions to the GUARD to untie the prisoner. The GUARD takes out a short dagger and cuts the rope.

NUR MOHAMMED
(To the guard)

Raise the dog's right arm.
(He turns his face eastwards)
Bismillah!

With stunning swiftness NUR MOHAMMED draws his sword and chops the extended arm off. ALI AKBAR squeals in pain as the arm flies through the air. There are groans, sounds of anguish, revulsion and hysteria. The stage is momentarily bathed in a red glow. MURAD ALI is shocked. He takes a large gulp from his goblet.

NUR MOHAMMED
(Glaring at GULAM ALI)

49

Majesty, were it not for the cowardly dogs who infect this Court with their influence, I would cut off the head of every non-believer in the name of Allah, the Compassionate, the Merciful who gave the Prophet Mohamed, peace be upon him, the eternal gift of the Holy Quran.

> *GULAM ALI reacts like a man who has been struck a low blow. MURAD ALI tries to regain his composure.*

MURAD ALI
(Weakly)

Contain your zeal! Enough damage has been done. No more talk of violence, it sickens me!

> *Two GUARDS enter to take the squealing ALI AKBAR away. Another GUARD retrieves the chopped off arm and hurries off.*

> *MURAD ALI starts to cough violently. There is mass confusion as he sways and is about to fall off the throne.*

BEGUM MUMTAZ
(Offstage, from behind the screen)

Leave, everybody, leave! My dearest father, what have they done to you?

> *The ATTENDANTS help MURAD ALI offstage. All OTHERS on stage depart hurriedly. NUR MOHAMMED stands alone. A spotlight is focused on his hard face. A solitary drum begins a slow rhythmic beat.*

END OF ACT I

SCENE 2

ACT I

SCENE 3

ACT I
SCENE 3

SETTING: *The scene is set in the same Durbar Hall, moments after MURAD ALI and all others have exited.*

BEGUM MUMTAZ enters from behind the screen. Her walk is slow and deliberate. A spotlight highlights her as she walks towards her husband, NUR MOHAMMED. Her face is lightly veiled. Her attire consists of a shimmering crimson two-piece gown. She slowly lifts the veil to display a beautiful face. She is the quintessential dark-eyed eastern beauty.

The Drumbeat stops.

NUR MOHAMMED
(Darkly)
How long must I wait! He can no longer manage the affairs of State. He must be done away with.

BEGUM MUMTAZ
(Outraged)
He is my father. I love him dearly. I wish no harm to come to him. He has given me all that I have wanted. You know that soon he will make you king. Be patient beloved. The throne is yours and after you our son.

NUR MOHAMMED
(Raising his voice)
I have waited for too long. Things are not the same. The Hindus of Sindh have the British to whom they increasingly turn for support. You can see it in their open friendship in

Court. That Hindu dog Hotchand and his son Seth Naomal grow bolder every day. Your drunken father, the miserable fool, encouraged by that dog, that Hindu sympathizer - that apostate - that Gulam Ali! He has put not only the kingdom at risk, he has endangered the cause of Islam.

(He softens)

For the sake of Sindh, for the sake of Islam, let us kill him tonight. He is so drunk he would feel no pain.

BEGUM MUMTAZ

Have you not spilled enough blood today, my Lord! You dare talk to me about killing my father! He agreed to our marriage despite others who sought my hand, who would have created stronger alliances with our kingdom – but for me.

(Warmly)

I chose you above all others. My father has denied me nothing and now you wish to kill him. Tomorrow your son will wish the same of you. Shall I then plot with his wives to depose you?

NUR MOHAMMED

(His voice rising)

My son! You say my son will plot to overthrow me! Leave it! Leave it! That he will be a schemer with his wives to wrench the throne from me. Ha! What a wondrous prospect! Throughout the ages that has been the way.

(Sarcastically)

I pray for that momentous occasion.

(He thunders)

Look at me, woman! Stop the fantasy! Leave it! Leave it! I have no son! For ten long years I have patiently waited, taken no other wives, and what have you given me! Three still-births and a sickly daughter who did not last till nightfall! Your womb madam is as fertile as the Thar Desert. Not all the herbs, potions, lotions, notions in the world nor all our prayers to Allah will change that which has been ordained by Allah Himself! Leave it! Leave it!

BEGUM MUMTAZ
(Sobbing)

Ya Allaha!

NUR MOHAMMED

Look at me, childless Princess of Sindh! Do you know what they call me at the Palace?
(He yells)
Mir Hijra, The Prince of Eunuchs, that is what they call me! Your Father in a drunken stupor told the Court Jester that he could never make me king, for I have yet to prove that I am a man.

MURAD ALI
(OffStage.)

He who cannot sire an heir can never rule a kingdom.

NUR MOHAMMED's face is contorted with rage. BEGUM MUMTAZ tries to embrace him. She turns her tear-stained face towards him and tenderly strokes his hair.

BEGUM MUMTAZ
(Tearfully)

You are king for me and we will have a son who will also be king. I believe that in my heart and Allah will not deny me that which my heart desires.

NUR MOHAMMED

Leave it! Leave it Woman! I can no longer stand your holy ramblings!

BEGUM MUMTAZ
(Softly)

My lord, I have been promised that a month to the day on his return from his pilgrimage to Mecca, a son will be born to us, a healthy prince who shall become the king of Sindh.

NUR MOHAMMED

Stop these fantasies at once Woman!

BEGUM MUMTAZ

Babaji, the keeper of the Crocodiles has assured me that it is written.

NUR MOHAMMED

I shall never have a son and all the holy men in the world cannot change the will of Allah!

> *NUR MOHAMED pushes BEGUM MUMTAZ away. She falls. He draws his sword from the scabbard. She lies there with her face turned away. There is utter silence. She raises her head exposing a tear-stained face. She sits up supporting her head on her raised knee. She hums a mournful tune. She is in a dream world, oblivious of the danger to her person. The humming becomes words uttered softly, as the accompanying somber music begins.*

BEGUM MUMTAZ
(Singing)

THE CHILD IN ME IS CRYING

LET ME GO, SET ME FREE,

HOW LONG MUST I ENDURE

THIS GRIEF, THIS MISERY?

(Tearfully)

THE CHILD IN ME IS SCREAMING

SAVE MY SOUL, RESCUE ME,

THIS STRANGE DARK WORLD IS NOT MY HOME,

THESE CREATURES PHANTOMS BE.

TAKE ME AWAY, LORD,

TAKE ME AWAY.

TAKE ME AWAY FROM THIS MISERABLE PLACE,

I'LL NEVER LEAVE,

I'LL NEVER STRAY,

SHOW ME THY FACE,

A HINT OF THY GRACE,

A CLUE TO THE PLACE,

SHOW ME,

PRAY SHOW ME THY FACE.

THEY CALL THEMSELVES MY LOVERS,

ALL THEIR VOWS ARE BRITTLE GLASS,

THEIR GIFTS ARE ASH AND DUST AND WORSE,

THEIR TRUTHS, THEIR LIES, ONE TANGLED MASS.

THE CHILD IN ME IS CRYING,

LET ME GO, SET ME FREE,

HOW LONG MUST I ENDURE,

THIS GRIEF, THIS MISERY,

TAKE ME AWAY LORD,

TAKE ME AWAY,

TAKE ME AWAY FROM THIS MISERABLE PLACE,

I'LL NEVER LEAVE,

I'LL NEVER STRAY,

PRAY SHOW ME THY FACE,

A HINT OF THY GRACE,

A CLUE TO THE PLACE,

LORD SHOW ME,

PRAY SHOW ME THY FACE.

TAKE ME AWAY.

NUR MOHAMMED looks at her tenderly. He sheaths his sword. He helps BEGUM MUMTAZ up and embraces her. She snuggles up to comfort him.

BEGUM MUMTAZ

My King! My Lord!

NUR MOHAMMED
(Defeated)

Leave it! Leave it! You cannot change my fate or yours any more than you can change the color of the skies or regulate the heat of the sun.

BEGUM MUMTAZ

My Lord! Why speak of changing the color of the sky and all else that Allah has created for your pleasure. I would stop at nothing to please you, to give you what your heart desires. My soul, my mind, my body are yours. You are my king.
(She cradles his head)
Come my king. Sit on this throne that is your birthright.

BEGUM MUMTAZ leads him to the throne. NUR MOHAMED furtively looks about. He sits guardedly at the edge. She eases him onto the throne. He sits back, a look of momentary triumph on his face. She sits at the foot of the throne, puts her head on his lap. She plays with his chest.

The lights dim. A blue shaft of light comes through the open window.

BEGUM MUMTAZ

Look My Lord! The moon is full tonight. The gift from Mecca that Babaji spoke of. Now is the time my Lord. Quick my Lord, upon this throne I shall make thee a King. A king shall be conceived tonight! Fill my womb now my Lord, as the moonlight fills this room.

She rearranges her long flowing hair. She straddles him.

BEGUM MUMTAZ

Now my Lord, quick. Now is the moment, enter me now.

Spot lights illuminate their faces. They are in the throes of passion. They move smoothly together to the sounds of quarrelling cats, the howls of jackals, the urgent chirpings of a hundred scattering birds, the crash of angry waves against rocky shores and the roars of a lion.

BEGUM MUMTAZ
(Breathlessly)
Death to all who come between me and my Lord.

NUR MOHAMMED
(Gasping)
Death! No mercy! Death to the Hindus! Death! Death! Death! Death to the British. Kill all infidels!

BEGUM MUMTAZ
Poison their wells!

NUR MOHAMMED
Piss in their wells! May that Hindu Hotchand burn in the everlasting fires of Hell! May his son Naomal and those British infidels perish. Curse that apostate Gulam Ali and his kin. May our son banish infidels from this our land. May he spread the Word of Allah throughout the world!

BEGUM MUMTAZ
(Screams in ecstasy)
Allah! Allah!

NUR MOHAMMED
Allah! Allah!

MUMTAZ & NUR MOHAMMED
(In unison)
Allah! Allah! Allah!

VOICES
(Off Stage.) *(In harmony)*
Allah! Allah!

The lights on stage start to fade. Voices offstage continue repeating "Allah".

[BLACKOUT]

END OF ACT I

SCENE 3

ACT II

SCENE 1

ACT II
SCENE 1

SETTING: A section of the main bazaar in Karachi, a seaport in the kingdom of Sindh. The backdrop of the set consists of billowy sails, fishnets and a doorway to a mosque.

Harmonious voices offstage, chanting Allah from the previous scene merge with the end of the afternoon prayers being offered at the mosque in the bazaar.

The stage is littered with the usual remnants, typical of eastern markets after the hectic morning commerce has abated.

The bright lighting on stage suggests the approach of the noon hour.

A group of veiled WOMEN in austere black chadors huddle together and make their way across the stage. Two URCHINS clown about. A SWEEPER is sweeping away debris with a long-handled broom. Two MUSLIMS are in animated but inaudible conversation by the doorway of the mosque.

Enter MOHAN, (12) accompanied by RAMJI, (60). The ash markings on RAMJI's forehead and his clothes identify him as a Hindu Brahmin. MOHAN notices the urchins horsing around. He pauses and comes to a halt. RAMJI continues to walk and tugs at MOHAN impatiently.

MOHAN
(Sullenly)
I am tired and wish to rest for a few moments.

RAMJI

You cannot be tired when I am not tired.

MOHAN
(Rudely)
Let go off my hand. I've listened to your blabbering nonsense all morning. I want to stay a while and play with those boys.
(He shouts))
Let me go, you old turtle!

RAMJI resists as MOHAN struggles.

RAMJI

Scoundrel, if I didn't know better, I would have thought that your father had raised you in the gutters and your mother washes your mouth in the sewers of Karachi. A sound thrashing is what you need before a holy word of Sanskrit is taught to you.

RAMJI slaps MOHAN on the back of his head.

RAMJI

Repeat after me the mantra I taught you this morning, 'Om Namah Shivaya, 'Om Namah Shivaya', repeat it, ungainly clod!

MOHAN manages to break loose. He runs behind the few remaining stalls. He is joined by the laughing URCHINS. The two MUSLIMS lingering by the doorway of the mosque notice the prancing MOHAN and the URCHINS teasing RAMJI. The two MUSLIMS huddle as though they have formulated a plan.

63

MUSLIM #1

Is this old turtle bothering you, lad?

MOHAN

He beats me all the time. My father thinks this old camel will make me a Hindu scholar. Bah! I'd learn more from the croaking of the frogs on the banks of the River Indus than from this slobbering old fool.

The two MUSLIMS laugh with delight.

MUSLIM #2

We can arrange it so that this old fool bothers you no more. Would you like to come with us?

MOHAN

First, I wish to play with my new friends - but where will you take me?

MUSLIM #1
(He points to the mosque)

In there!

(He laughs ominously)

A Muslim enters from the doorway of the mosque and joins the two men.

MOHAN

What's inside there?

MUSLIM #2

It's as cool as the inside of a pomegranate! The air is filled with the perfume of a thousand flowers! There is a fountain of sparkling sherbet!

RAMJI

What! Have you no shame? You dare seduce a Hindu boy to enter your mosque. I am his custodian and obliged to return him to his parents. I am answerable to his father for his safety. Go about your own business and let me tend to mine.

MUSLIM #3

(He approaches RAMJI menacingly)

Listen Teacher! We would drag you in as well, only we do not wish to pollute our hallowed mosque with your presence. Be off with you and when you get home tell your wife to carve up a cow and cook you up a dish of beef curry!

RAMJI

I will not waste my holy breath arguing on the roadside with hooligans. Come Mohan, it is late. We must hurry home.

MUSLIM #1

Be on your way old man, the boy comes with us.

The MUSLIMS violently shove RAMJI aside and take MOHAN by the arm in the direction of the mosque. MOHAN turns and sees RAMJI fall and scream.

MOHAN

(Frightened)

Don't hurt him, please, he means no harm!

RAMJI rises.

RAMJI

Help! Help! They have kidnapped a little boy. Against all reason, they have taken an innocent Hindu boy inside their mosque. Help! A tragedy worse than death is going to occur. Help! Somebody, please help!

> *Enter a group of LOCALS. They begin to take sides. Some voices are demanding the release of the boy. Someone in the crowd hurls a stone. Pandemonium breaks out.*

> *NAOMAL comes rushing in with some others.*

NAOMAL
(To a companion)
Quick dispatch a messenger to Ahmad Bugree. Tell him to come quickly with his constables for the crowd gets more restless every minute.

> *MUSLIMS come pouring out of the mosque. HINDUS enter from all directions. They stand in separate groups and prepare for battle.*

A HINDU
Death to the Muslims! We won't take it anymore!

NAOMAL
(To the Hindus)
Calm down! Calm down!

A HINDU
Kill the Muslims who kidnap our children, rape our women, burn our shops.

A MUSLIM
Piss on you, you filthy Hindu dogs!

NAOMAL
(To the Hindus)

My brothers, no good will come from violence.

A HINDU

We are forced to respond to violence with violence since nothing else works!

NAOMAL

This puts all our families in grave danger.

A HINDU

I am Gobind, son of Parsram. With the help of only ten other Hindus, we fought twenty of these cowardly bastards when they stole sheep from our herds.
(He weeps)
They raped my twelve-year-old daughter and with the whole village watching in terror, they threw my son to the ground.
(He sobs)
He had just turned fourteen, they cut his..., disfigured him with a knife. The boy was so ashamed he ran away from home and joined the People of the Night.

RAMJI

Please no more talk. Help me! They will do that to little Mohan inside the mosque.

A MUSLIM

There are no Hindus in our mosque. He may have been an infidel when he entered, but soon he will be one of the faith.

A blood curdling scream is heard from the Mosque.

A HINDU

You sons of pigs who wallow in waste will pay. Death to the Muslims! May you all go to Hell! Is this behavior also prescribed in your Quran?

A MUSLIM

Rally, oh true believers! The infidels have denigrated the holiest of the Holy. The sacred Book has been defiled!

ANOTHER MUSLIM

Arise O Muslims! Kill the Hindu serpents who grow bolder every day because of the cunning English wolves who support them!

ANOTHER MUSLIM

Kill the infidel English as well.

> *The CROWD on stage gyrate in rhythm as drums beat. The Music begins solemnly as the dance of death commences.*

> *HINDUS and MUSLIMS are face to face with each other. They move in rhythm as they jostle for advantage.*

> *An eerie scream is returned by the MUSLIMS in response to a yell from the HINDUS as they poise for engagement.*

> *NAOMAL with two of his COMPANIONS exits the stage. The lights dim. The music gets louder.*

A MUSLIM
(Sings, in a loud clear voice.)

ALLAH!

LORD OF LORDS,

KING OF KINGS,

GOD OF GODS!

BISMILLAH!

WE WILL FIGHT,

TOOTH AND NAIL,

FOR OUR GOD!

(chorus by other MUSLIMS)

WE WILL FIGHT TO THE DEATH FOR YOUR NAME,

WE WILL KILL AND DESTROY AND WE'LL MAIM,

ALL OF THOSE WHO WILL NOT PLAY THE GAME,

AND ACKNOWLEDGE

THE GLORY OF YOUR NAME.

A HINDU
(sings in a loud clear voice)

BRAHMA!

LORD OF LORDS,

KING OF KINGS,

GOD OF GODS!

(Joined by other HINDUS)

SHIVA!

WE WILL FIGHT TOOTH AND NAIL

FOR OUR GODS!

MUSLIMS and HINDUS
(sing in unison)

WE WILL FIGHT TO THE DEATH FOR YOUR NAME,

WE WILL KILL AND DESTROY AND WE'LL MAIM,

ALL OF THOSE WHO WILL NOT PLAY THE GAME,

AND ACKNOWLEDGE THE GLORY OF YOUR NAME.

Enter BABAJI, dressed in his black robe. He fearlessly weaves his way in between the battle lines. His right arm is raised skyward.

BABAJI
(Sings)

WHAT A SHAME!

WHAT A SHAME!

WHAT A SHAME!

WHAT WE DO TO EACH OTHER FOR A NAME!

MUSLIMS

ALLAH!

LORD OF LORDS,

KING OF KINGS,

GOD OF GODS.

BISMILLAH!

WE WILL FIGHT,

TOOTH AND NAIL

FOR OUR GOD.

WE WILL FIGHT TO THE DEATH

FOR YOUR NAME,

WE WILL KILL AND DESTROY AND WE'LL MAIM,

ALL THOSE WHO WILL NOT PLAY THE GAME,

AND ACKNOWLEDGE THE GLORY OF YOUR NAME.

HINDUS

BRAHMA!

LORD OF LORDS,

KING OF KINGS,

GOD OF GODS,

SHIVA!

WE WILL FIGHT TOOTH AND NAIL

FOR OUR GODS,

WE WILL FIGHT TO THE DEATH

FOR YOUR NAME,

WE WILL KILL AND DESTROY, AND WE'LL MAIM,

ALL OF THOSE WHO WILL NOT PLAY THE GAME,

AND ACKNOWLEDGE THE GLORY OF YOUR NAME!

BABAJI meanders with his right hand pointing skywards.

BABAJI

WHAT A SHAME!

WHAT A SHAME!

WHAT A SHAME!

WHAT WE DO TO EACH OTHER FOR A NAME!

Enter a MUSLIM, carrying a Quran in one hand and a fiery torch in the other. He zigzags through the battle lines.

THE MUSLIM
Islam is in Danger! Arise O Muslims! Defend the Faith!

As the song and dance progresses the lighting dims. Within moments a red strobe light highlights the action and accentuates the glint of blades.

All on stage rhythmically rise, crouch and fall.

The accompanying sounds include gasps, ejaculations of pain and anguish amidst sporadic utterances of "Allah" and "Brahma".

The song is sung with passion, and the dance performed with energy and vigor.

BABAJI intervenes, repeating his lines as the MUSLIM carrying the book and the fiery torch meanders through the dancers several times.

The singing and dancing winds down.

Red spotlights flicker to reveal the fallen victims.

Sounds of human agony are accompanied by the occasional utterances of "Allah!" and "Brahma!"

A solitary drum beat simulates the rhythm of a heartbeat.

In the background sporadic flames indicate a spreading fire.

The MUSLIM carrying the book and the fiery torch exits.

A spotlight reveals BABAJI sitting centerstage with his right hand pointed skywards, as he surveys the carnage.

The solitary drum continues its mournful beat as the lights fade.

[BLACKOUT]

END OF ACT II

SCENE 1

ACT II

SCENE 2

ACT II
SCENE 2

The solitary drum beat continues from the previous scene. It morphs into the sound of urgent and loud knocking and pounding. The Stage is dark.

CAPTAIN OF THE KING'S GUARD
(OffStage)

I am the Captain of the king's guard. Who dares seek entry in His Majesty's private apartments at this time of night!

ANOTHER MALE VOICE
(OffStage)

Open the door! Her Royal Highness, Begum Mumtaz is here and demands entry.

CAPTAIN
(OffStage)

I have orders that His Majesty is not to be disturbed for any reason. With respect, the noble princess will understand that His Majesty has been unwell for several days and is resting.

BEGUM MUMTAZ
(OffStage)

Captain, I desire to see His Majesty now on a matter that cannot wait till morning. You will either open this door or I will order it broken down and thereafter the first head that will roll will be yours. Make your choice now.

The door is heard opening.

CAPTAIN
(OffStage)

Your Highness, I fear I have disobeyed my King, and displeased you as well!

BEGUM MUMTAZ
(OffStage)

You shall remain blameless in this matter Captain. I will see to it. I will announce myself.

THE SETTING: KING MURAD ALI'S bedchambers. The bed is at centerstage. It is massive and low and covered with fine crimson and gold fabric. A table with a silver jug and goblets is close to the bed. A hookah and another low table adorned with fruits and flowers sit on the other side of the bed. Persian rugs cover the floors. The walls are adorned with silk. The Lighting emits a soft pink hazy glow.

There are movements from under the bed covers.

Enter BEGUM MUMTAZ. She wears an emerald green gown. Her beautiful face is unveiled. She carries a small Quran and a candle. She places the book and the candle on the table.

BEGUM MUMTAZ
Father! Father! Wake up!

MURAD ALI
(His head emerges from under the bed covers)

What! What! How can this be! Who dares disturb me at this time of night when even the poorest of my subjects enjoy a night's rest from the labors of the day!

BEGUM MUMTAZ

It is I, Mumtaz, and I have come here to tell you dearest father that all of Sindh is in flames, from the Khyber to the seaport of Karachi. The river Indus has turned red with the blood of our Muslim brothers and sisters - blood spilled by hordes of Hindu murderers led by your pretended friend Hotchand and his cursed offspring Naomal. Their boldness stems from their unholy alliance with the infidel English dogs who covet Sindh.

MURAD ALI

(Takes a gulp of wine)

Each day you sound more like your husband. Have we not the laws to deal with these events? Have we no civil authorities, appointed officials, no armed forces? Must I be the one to deal with every petty disturbance in the kingdom?

BEGUM MUMTAZ

(Dramatically)

Arise! Arise, O beloved father. It is time to put down the goblet and take up the sword. I have here with me the Holy Quran. Islam and the kingdom are in danger. I beg you to take an oath upon the holiest of books, that you will cleanse our land of non-believers who kill our brothers and flaunt our most sacred customs. My husband and I have issued a firmament for the arrest of Seth Hotchand and Seth Naomal on charges of blasphemy, insurrection, treason and murder.

MURAD ALI

(Agitated)

How dare you! Have you both lost your senses? I don't need this at this time of night! Get out! Get out!

MURAD ALI thumps his bed in rage. From under the ample bed covers, two GIRLS appear. They struggle fearfully to cover themselves with the bedcovers.

MURAD ALI
(To the girls)
No, not you. You stay here!

He shoves the GIRLS back under the bedcovers. BEGUM MUMTAZ turns away and shakes her head in disbelief. Slowly she regains her composure.

MURAD ALI
How dare you enter my bedchambers at night! I am the King and your husband and you issue royal commands! I knew no good would come from indulging you all these years. Are you not satisfied that you run the palace as though it were your own fiefdom, that now you and your hate-filled impotent husband have taken to meddling in matters of State as well!

BEGUM MUMTAZ
Don't say that! Father it is I who has been unable to bear children. Father, the blood flows freely as we speak. You need to put a stop to it! In the name of Allah, you must uphold the laws of the kingdom.

MURAD ALI
I forbid you to speak such nonsense.

BEGUM MUMTAZ
Take an oath upon the sacred Quran Father, that you will endorse the warrants we have issued. Seth Naomal and Seth Hotchand supply the English with grains, transport and other provisions. There is a shortage of the basic commodities in the

bazaars, and while our people starve and struggle to survive, the English intruders bring more and more soldiers into their camps and want for nothing. The riots are starting to weaken your authority, father. If you do not act now, the kingdom will be lost! The English have been waiting for this opportunity to seize control.

> *MUMTAZ approaches MURAD ALI and tenderly nuzzles her head in his shoulder. The two GIRLS leave as they cover themselves with their garments.*

BEGUM MUMTAZ

In the name of Allah, dearest father, we must waste no further time. If you would only permit my husband to supervise the return of law and order in the realm, I know that calm will be restored in the streets in no time.

MURAD ALI
(Looks towards the door and calls out)
Summon my worthy cousin Gulam Ali!
(To BEGUM MUMTAZ)
It is his responsibility to counsel me on these matters.

BEGUM MUMTAZ

And what of my husband? Why do you treat him with such cruelty? He is the heir apparent and yet you fawn on Gulam Ali, that lover of Hindu dogs, that faithless scoundrel who deserts the cause of Islam again and again. Why, Father, why?

> *Enter GULAM ALI immaculately dressed. He is accompanied by two OFFICERS. He bows to BEGUM MUMTAZ and MURAD ALI.*

GULAM ALI

Majesty, there is much trouble about the realm. I have issued summons to Seth Hotchand and Seth Naomal to return to Hyderabad under the protection of my personal guards.

BEGUM MUMTAZ

So they return to the palace as conquering heroes, as equals of His Majesty to negotiate terms of peace! You, you...weakling! You sap! You imbecile!

GULAM ALI
(He bows to BEGUM MUMTAZ and addresses MURAD ALI)

I also issued a request to Seth Hotchand and to Seth Naomal to participate in a joint appeal to Hindus to stay indoors and refrain from all acts of violence. Seth Hotchand has sent word that he is willing to do so and is on his way here.
(He glances over at BEGUM MUMTAZ)
Unfortunately, a few hours ago it was reported to me that a warrant was issued for the arrest of Seth Hotchand and Seth Naomal. The news of this has only added to more bitter and bloody clashes in all parts of the kingdom.

BEGUM MUMTAZ
(To GULAM ALI)

You are not a Muslim. You are a spineless lover of infidels. It is your disastrous policy of appeasement that has weakened the kingdom. For over sixty years the Talpur family has ruled this country by the sword, and the laws dictated by the Quran. Now because of your misguided counsel, we have the Hindu dogs killing our Muslim brothers, defying our edicts and defiling our mosques.

GULAM ALI

(He ignores the outburst. He addresses MURAD ALI)

I have invited the respected Babaji, the Keeper of the Sacred Crocodiles to act as sole Arbitrator. He enjoys the respect and confidence of both Hindus and Muslims of Sindh. He has agreed to the commission and has joined me in issuing injunctions to Hindus and Muslims to immediately withdraw from all acts of revenge and retaliation.

BEGUM MUMTAZ

(Hysterically)

Why was my husband not consulted! This is an affront to his position! A departure from tradition and an insult to our beloved Talpur ancestors.

MURAD ALI

Enough. No more! I will not permit this poisonous prattle any longer.

MURAD ALI takes a gulp from his goblet. Suddenly he clutches his chest. His face is twisted with pain. He heaves for air. He falls back on his pillows gasping for breath.

BEGUM MUMTAZ screams and rushes towards Murad Ali. Confusion breaks out as COURTIERS and ATTENDANTS enter and exit in panic.

GULAM ALI

Summon Dr. Burnes. Bring the English doctor here forthwith!

BEGUM MUMTAZ

Oh, my beloved father! Allah save him! Please don't take him now!

BEGUM MUMTAZ is in the throes of grief.

Wake up dearest father! Open your eyes. Say something. Someone do something! Ya Allaha!

> *DR. BURNES enters and examines MURAD ALI's lifeless body. He shakes his head with resignation.*
>
> *KING MURAD ALI is dead.*
>
> *GULAM ALI holds the dead monarch's hand. He bends and kisses it.*
>
> *Enter NUR MOHAMMED as all in the room bow reverently.*

COURT OFFICIAL

May Allah receive Mir Murad Ali in Paradise. Long Live Mir Nur Mohammed, Regent of Sindh!

ANOTHER COURT OFFICIAL

It is the will of Allah! Glory to Nur Mohammed, Regent of Sindh and Defender of the Faith! May he live a thousand years!

BEGUM MUMTAZ.
(Dazed)

Father! My beloved father! The breath has left your body and I am lifeless!

> *Silent vows of allegiance to the new king are being made by all in the room.*
>
> *NUR MOHAMMED's eyes are focused on GULAM ALI.*
>
> *With dignity GULAM ALI approaches NUR MOHAMMED and bows at the waist.*

GULAM ALI.

I have always served at the pleasure of my King.

He bows and exits.

NUR MOHAMMED
(To an OFFICER)

Slaughter him! I want soldiers out on the streets, and in the name of Allah and the Prophet Mohammed, may Peace be upon Him, kill every Hindu in Sindh - except Seth Hotchand and his son Seth Naomal. Bring them here alive. If you are unable to bring them here, do the needful. Remember, finish the business there. All Hindu homes and businesses are to be left standing. All their possessions are herewith made the property of our realm. Burn their temples to the ground, smash the idols of their false Gods until they are as fine as the powdered sands of our deserts.

NUR MOHAMMED stares at the silver jug and the goblets.

NUR MOHAMMED

Take that poison away.

An ATTENDANT rushes forward to retrieve the tray and exits.

COURTIER

Death to the British as well. Let us kill every Englishman who resides within our King's domains.

NUR MOHAMMED
(Points to DR. BURNES)

We will start with this one – but put him in chains for now. We will dispatch this infidel to Allah in good time.

A shaken DR. BURNES is led out of the room.

NUR MOHAMMED

From this moment on, all past treaties with the English dogs are null and void. Islam is in danger. Defend the faith and in the name of Allah and the Prophet Mohamed – may peace be upon him - let the wailing begin.

Enter WOMEN dressed in white Chadors, wailing and beating their breasts. BEGUM MUMTAZ is draped in white by the mourners. She joins in the wailing. The stage darkens. A single spotlight focuses on NUR MOHAMMED. The beating of drums with cries of 'Allah', 'Death to the English' and 'Death to the Hindus' accompany the wailing.

END OF ACT II

SCENE 2

ACT II

SCENE 3

ACT II
SCENE 3

SETTING: *As the lights gradually brighten, the stage reveals the Karachi bazaar area where the riot had broken out in Act 2 Scene 1.*

The wailing continues from the previous scene.

The HINDUS on stage invoke the names of 'Rama' 'Shiva', 'Krishna',

The MUSLIMS on stage make anxious pleas to 'Allah' and the Prophet Mohammed.

Clouds of smoke puff from the ruins of the burnt down mosque.

Wailing women and screaming children search through the rubble for their kin.

SETH HOTCHAND
(Sadly)

This is madness.

SETH HINDUJA

It has spread like a wildfire all over Sindh. Every village and town is up in arms.

SETH HINDUJA

Tell me this is a nightmare and that it will pass when I awake.

SETH HOTCHAND

The stench of burning flesh is real enough. The sounds of pain that fill the air is no illusion. The senses revolt at the sight of these tangled remains of Hindus and Muslims. I must leave at once for Hyderabad. We must work together to put an end to this.

SETH HINDUJA

The roads are not safe for travel. Roving gangs are attacking caravans, killing indiscriminately and looting whatever they can carry. Perhaps you should leave in a few days when things are a bit calmer.

SETH HOTCHAND

So many of our young lay waste in the streets.

Enter some LOCALS who help the wounded off the stage.

Enter an OFFICER and SOLDIERS bearing the Sindh colors.

The OFFICER approaches SETH HOTCHAND. He reads from a document.

OFFICER

This is a summons issued by Prince Gulam Ali, Prime Minister of Sindh, and duly bears his seal. You, Seth Hotchand are to accompany me under armed escort to the palace in Hyderabad along with your son, Seth Naomal, to assist His Majesty's Government to restore law and order in the kingdom. Sir, if you wish to retain the favor of His Majesty, you will surrender yourself and your son Seth Naomal to the dictates of this summons.

SETH HINDUJA

The road to Hyderabad is strewn with dead bodies. Thieves and murderers roam freely. Surely you know he will be killed before he gets there.

OFFICER
(Impatiently)
I have my orders. We must start immediately while there is light.

SETH HOTCHAND

I will come with you without hesitation.

SETH HINDUJA

Seth Hotchand, we will accompany you to tell His Majesty of the truth.

There is loud support of this from the HINDUS on Stage.

A MUSLIM
(To SETH HINDUJA)
I will slice your mother's throat, Hindu dog!

OFFICER
(To the Muslim)
Hold it. I have orders to bring Seth Hotchand to Hyderabad alive and unharmed. That is the Prime Minister's express command.
(To HOTCHAND)
Do you think that His Majesty's personal guards will be unable to protect you?

Enter three more SOLDIERS and a CAPTAIN of the Hyderabad Court accompanied by a motley crowd of

RUFFIANS led by the earless, one-armed ALI AKBAR.
He spits in HOTCHAND'S face.

ALI AKBAR
(Pointing to HOTCHAND)
This is the infidel who consorts with the English dogs. He started the trouble and fans the flames of hate against our brothers in Islam. He spat on the holy book.

CAPTAIN
(To the OFFICER)
King Murad Ali has been admitted within the pearly gates of Paradise and has received the blessings of Allah. In the name of King Nur Mohammed, now Regent of Sindh, you are relieved of your orders.
(To HOTCHAND)
I have a warrant here. I am ordered to arrest you and your son Seth Naomal on charges of treason and blasphemy.

The Hindus and Muslims in the crowds begin to get restless.

A HINDU
Seth Hotchand do not go. They are bent on injustice.

ANOTHER HINDU
You will never make it to Hyderabad alive. Even if you do, false witnesses will be brought against you.
(He yells)
Death to the Muslims!

A MUSLIM
Kill the Hindu dogs.

HINDUS and MUSLIMS shove and push each other.

The CAPTAIN grabs HOTCHAND.

CAPTAIN
(To a SOLDIER)
We must act fast. We may not be able to take him. Let us finish the business here and now.
(He smirks and says to HOTCHAND)
You are about to receive a special gift from his Royal Highness King Nur Mohammed.
(To the SOLDIERS)
Seize him!

The SOLDIERS surround HOTCHAND and carry him centerstage.

They pin his arms and legs. The Captain approaches HOTCHAND with a knife.

A spotlight reveals the Captains face.

CAPTAIN
Do not worry Seth Hotchand, I will not kill you, for that would be a waste. Instead, I shall be rewarded in Paradise for having rescued your immortal soul.

The CAPTAIN laughs. The MUSLIMS crowd about HOTCHAND and yell cheerful encouragement. The HINDUS scream in horror. The crowd get closer to HOTCHAND's body which lies spread-eagled and face up. He is overpowered by the SOLDIERS as he struggles to free himself.

CAPTAIN
(To the Soldiers)
Strip him from the waist down. Now!

HINDUS AND HOTCHAND
(Chant the Mantra)
OM NAMAH SHIVAYA! OM NAMAH SHIVAYA!

The CAPTAIN faces East, and draws a knife.

CAPTAIN
Receive into thy fold, O Almighty Allah, one more Believer!

The knife disappears from view, obscured by the surrounding SOLDIERS. HOTCHAND groans as the CAPTAIN raises the knife.

CAPTAIN
Now he is one of the Faith.

The stage lights turn red.

Somber voices chant Om Namah Shivaya softly.

MUSLIMS
(Sing)

ALLAH!

LORD OF LORDS,

KING OF KINGS,

GOD OF GODS.

BISMILLAH!

WE WILL FIGHT, TOOTH AND NAIL

FOR OUR GOD.

WE WILL FIGHT TO THE DEATH FOR YOUR NAME,

WE WILL KILL AND DESTROY AND WE'LL MAIM,

ALL OF THOSE WHO WILL NOT PLAY THE GAME,

AND ACKNOWLEDGE THE GLORY OF YOUR NAME.

HINDUS

BRAHMA!

LORD OF LORDS,

KING OF KINGS,

GOD OF GODS.

SHIVA!

WE WILL FIGHT TOOTH AND NAIL FOR OUR GODS,

(HINDUS AND MUSLIMS TOGETHER)

WE WILL FIGHT TO THE DEATH FOR YOUR NAME,

WE WILL KILL AND DESTROY AND WE'LL MAIM,

ALL THOSE WHO WILL NOT PLAY THE GAME,

AND ACKNOWLEDGE THE GLORY OF YOUR NAME.

MUSLIMS

ALLAH! LORD OF LORDS,

KING OF KINGS, GOD OF GODS.

BISMILLAH!

WE WILL FIGHT, TOOTH AND NAIL

FOR OUR GOD.

WE WILL FIGHT TO THE DEATH FOR YOUR NAME,

WE WILL KILL AND DESTROY AND WE'LL MAIM,

ALL Of THOSE WHO WILL NOT PLAY THE GAME,

AND ACKNOWLEDGE THE GLORY OF YOUR NAME.

HINDUS

BRAHMA! LORD OF LORDS,

KING OF KINGS,

GOD OF GODS.

SHIVA,

WE WILL FIGHT TOOTH AND NAIL FOR OUR GODS,

(HINDUS AND MUSLIMS TOGETHER)

WE WILL FIGHT TO THE DEATH FOR YOUR NAME,

WE WILL KILL AND DESTROY AND WE'LL MAIM,

ALL THOSE WHO WILL NOT PLAY THE GAME,

AND ACKNOWLEDGE THE GLORY OF YOUR NAME.

The Dance of Death enacted in the previous riot scene accompanies the singing. As bodies strike and fall, HINDUS and MUSLIMS exit the stage in panic, dragging some of the fallen bodies with them. As the singing continues the stage lights change to a pink sunset hue.

Enter BABAJI. *He sits beside Seth* HOTCHAND *and raises his right hand skywards.*

The Music stops. There is a moment of silence.

Enter NAOMAL. *He sits beside* BABAJI. NAOMAL *is overcome with grief.*

NAOMAL

My Father! Instruct me now for I am lost.

HOTCHAND

I have no desire to rejoin the world. I now wish to pass my days as a Sufi fakir. Do as you must my son.

BABAJI
(*to* NAOMAL *as he points to* HOTCHAND)

The reverend Pir Murad once said "It is better to restore one dead heart to eternal life than to give life to a thousand dead bodies."

Deep voices chant OM! The chant becomes louder.

Enter SHADOWY FIGURES. They crowd around HOTCHAND.

One of them offers him water from a canteen. Another offers him something to eat.

BABAJI

Behold Seth Hotchand! The People of the Night have come to welcome you. Arise Seth Hotchand. You are now one with them.

The People of the Night chant in unison.

OM NAMAH SHIVAYA,

OM NAMAH SHIVAYA,

OM NAMAH SHIVAYA,

OM NAMAH SHIVAYA,

OM!

HOTCHAND struggles to get up as NAOMAL helps him.

HOTCHAND and THE PEOPLE OF THE NIGHT exit the stage.

Offstage. The chant 'Om Namah Shivaya' continues.

A spotlight reveals BABAJI and NAOMAL sitting amidst the dead.

BABAJI raises his right hand skyward.

The Spotlight slowly fades as the stage is plunged into darkness.

Offstage. The sounds of galloping horses drown out the chanting voices.

END OF ACT II

SCENE 3

ACT III
SCENE 1

ACT III
SCENE 1

SETTING: It is late evening and the sounds of horses continue from the previous scene. The stage depicts a clearing in the lush green private forests of Sindh's Royal family.

COL. HENRY POTTINGER accompanied by CAPT. CARLESS (30) and a small group of BRITISH SAILORS and a few LOCALS are establishing camp after a hunt.

A Stag with magnificent antlers lies on the ground. Some of the LOCALS carry wood to start a fire.

POTTINGER

That was quite a hunt. Who would have guessed that sailors would have so much fun on land?

PETTY OFFICER

Aye Sir! Wait till I tell the missus back 'ome that I went 'unting in a bloody Rajah's forest.

CARLESS
(To Petty Officer)
I say Jones, get some of the boys to water down the horses.

PETTY OFFICER

Yessir.
(He yells)
OK. Lads, get one of Hasan's men to water down the horses.

ENGLISH SAILOR
(Offstage.)
Right-O Chief! Wash the horses, juldee! Come on, move 'fore I kick your black arse to Kandahar.

There is laughter offstage.

CARLESS
(To COL. POTTINGER)
There is nothing more exhilarating than riding a fine Arabian. It comes second only to being on the deck of a ship.

POTTINGER
Ah! Once a Navy man always a Navy man. It's the land and horses for me first, I always say.

HASAN
(OffStage. In Sindhi)
Arey Ali, hee madarchod Angrez chaitho ghodan khe parnee deh! Sahib, he will bring water. He will take good care of the horses. His father was a horse thief in Kabul and taught him all the tricks of the trade.

There is more laughter.

PETTY OFFICER
(Shouts)
Just you keep your eyes peeled boys. It's a long way back to the ship at Karachi. Tell these buggers they are going to have to carry us on their backs if the horses disappear.

SAILOR
(OffStage.)
Right-o Chief!

CARLESS

Who would suspect that this lush forest, filled with game would be found in the middle of a desert?

POTTINGER

Naomal once told me that the cultivators don't get enough fresh water for their crops, as most of it is diverted to maintain these royal game preserves.

PETTY OFFICER

The poor buggers all over India have the same kind of luck. The Rajah starves 'is people until one of his Queens does him in. An idiot son takes his place and does much the same.

POTTINGER

These are dangerous times. We have to be very careful. I've talked to Naomal's people all over Sindh. Nur Mohammed would kill every Englishman he can get his hands on.

CARLESS

I'm eager to return to our ship Sir, as soon as we can. This is a country of lootoos and thuggees if ever there was one.

PETTY OFFICER

You're right Sir. Can't be too careful in these parts. No sooner does a man turn 'is back when 'e feels a knife in it. I've seen it 'appen I 'ave. Why just the other day some of our men went to a place by the port where there were local lovelies to be 'ad. sort of a party for the price of a few bottles of rum. Turned out they were all men dressed like women and there were a few young boys too. I say, Sir, you never saw English sailors so enraged. Could 'ave turned ugly!

CARLESS

This is scandalous. Tell the men I'll have none of it. Lord knows there's enough to deal with here. Ahmad Bugree who runs Karachi is a character. He'd jump at the first chance of killing a few of us for any reason.

PETTY OFFICER

No cause for alarm Sir, the men have been told to stay away from the place. Most of them were too sauced at the time. Wouldn't be able to find the place again, I don't think!

(Offstage) Shots are fired as horses neigh restlessly. POTTINGER, CARLESS and SAILORS reach for their weapons.

POTTINGER

We are British Officers! How dare you attack our party! Your King will have your head for this!

There is more shouting and gunfire offstage. It stops as suddenly as it started.

Enter BUGREE, dressed as a Muslim nobleman escorted by some rough looking LOCALS

BUGREE

I am Lord Bugree, Governor of Karachi and the overseer of the King's forests. Whoever enters these forests does so only with my permission. You infidels have dared to enter and now be prepared to meet your Maker.

POTTINGER

I am Colonel Henry Pottinger, traveling with a fellow officer and men with special permission granted to us by the Court in Hyderabad.

CARLESS
How dare you threaten us?

BUGREE
Shut your mouth infidel or I will cut out your tongue and feed it to the desert lizards.

BUGREE whips out a knife and approaches CARLESS.

NAOMAL
(Offstage)
Should any harm come to the Englishmen, touch a hair on their heads, and we will dispatch you, Bugree, to the Land of Yama. I am Seth Naomal of Karachi, and with me here are five hundred Hindus who remember you well. They impatiently await my instructions. They will not have to wait much longer. We will do to you what you have done to us for so long. Today you will feel like a Hindu under the Talpur kings.

BUGREE
(Frightened)
Seth Naomal! Seth Naomal! Show mercy to a man who has only followed orders. I have saved many Hindus from the bad Muslims who are bent on mischief. I wish to do no harm to the Englishmen. Come to think of it, I like them.

NAOMAL
(Offstage)
Very well then. You have asked for mercy and you shall receive it. Return to Karachi but do not forget this night. Never return to this forest again, for it is now ours. Report that to your master at the palace in Hyderabad. Go before I change my mind because it will change your kismet.

BUGREE

Praise be to Allah, the Compassionate, the Merciful. May Allah bless you and yours, Seth Naomal.

He bows deeply to the Englishman.

BUGREE

Salaam Englishmen, we now take your leave. We did not mean to disturb you. Please enjoy.
(*To his MEN*)
Come men, let us return.

NAOMAL
(*Offstage.*)
It's a long walk to Karachi for you and your men. Our people will escort you to the edge of the forest. Your horses and camels will stay here with us. Rest assured that they will be put to good use.

BUGREE

The words were about to leave my lips when you mentioned it. Yes, yes, please keep the horses and the camels. It is our gift to you.

NAOMAL
(*OffStage*)
Thank you. We will also unburden you of the weapons you carry. It is so much wiser to travel light as we Hindus are advised to do, especially these days, when the roads are filled with lootoos and other unscrupulous persons.

BUGREE

I would have suggested that myself, only you mentioned it before I could! Such foresight!

The humbled BUGREE and his MEN disarm.

BUGREE

Give the Englishmen your salaams, fools!

> *BUGREE and his MEN scrape and bow as they exit the stage.*
>
> *Enter NAOMAL.*
>
> *Enter the PEOPLE OF THE NIGHT.*
>
> *The lighting suggests it is late evening.*
>
> *A bonfire is started.*
>
> *A large pot containing a beverage is set up.*
>
> *All on stage are drinking from donos, (cups made of leaves)*
>
> *NAOMAL stands with CAPTAIN CARLESS and COL. POTTINGER. NAOMAL raises a toast.*

NAOMAL

To our friends!

PEOPLE OF THE NIGHT

To our friends!

> *POTTINGER raises another toast.*

POTTINGER

In honor of all our comrades who have been killed by Nur Mohammed. People of the Night, I salute you!

> *The PEOPLE OF THE NIGHT cheer with gusto.*

POTTINGER

(To Naomal)

Your people informed us that we would find you here. We came under the pretext of a hunt, not realizing that we were the quarry. Thank you old friend. You came through again - only this time it wasn't a moment too soon.

NAOMAL

It was nothing Henry, you would have done as much yourself.

POTTINGER

Our real purpose was to make contact with you.

He removes his glove and offers it to NAOMAL.

POTTINGER

Seth Naomal, will you pick up the gauntlet?

NAOMAL accepts the glove and raises it above his head.

NAOMAL

I have picked up the gauntlet. People of the Night. Have we picked up the gauntlet?

PEOPLE OF THE NIGHT

(In Unison)

We have picked up the gauntlet.

A HINDU

Death to the Talpurs. Death to Nur Mohammed. To Hyderabad! To victory!

POTTINGER

General Charles Napier awaits our signal. He stands ready to enter Sindh at the head of the Bombay army.

CARLESS

Admiral Maitland, Commander of British Naval forces is steaming towards Karachi and is prepared to take over the port.

POTTINGER

Seth Naomal do you pledge your allegiance to the authority of British rule in Sindh?

NAOMAL

We stand with you Henry. We will fight alongside your troops to lift the yoke of tyranny from the bent backs of our countrymen. Do we welcome the British to Sindh?

PEOPLE OF THE NIGHT

We welcome our British friends!

POTTINGER

There will be sacrifices. Lives will be lost. We will continue to require food, water and other supplies.

NAOMAL

You shall have it.

POTTINGER

We will need horses, camels and storage facilities.

NAOMAL

All necessary provisions and facilities will be arranged for. We earnestly hope that private properties confiscated by the present government in Hyderabad will be returned to their rightful owners.

POTTINGER

That will be our first task.

NAOMAL

We pray that Hindu temples and all places of worship will be protected.

POTTINGER

And they shall. It is also our desire to take your counsel on all matters that will restore the rule of law in Sindh. Thereafter, we shall all work together to promote the welfare of this land and its inhabitants. Are we One?

NAOMAL

We are One.

POTTINGER

Gentlemen, we are about to undertake war and we have pledged our fidelity to each other, whatever the outcome.

Music begins softly.

PEOPLE OF THE NIGHT

OM! OM! OM!

NAOMAL

HOME, HOME, HOME.

THE PEOPLE OF THE NIGHT

OM! HOME!

NAOMAL

I AM ALL THE PEOPLE OF THE NIGHT,

CAN'T YOU SEE,

I LIVE AMIDST THE DARKENED BUSH

AND THE SHADOW OF THE TREE.

I'LL DRINK THE MILK OF CACTUS,

I'LL EAT THE DESERT SAND,

UNTIL THE WRATH OF BRAHMA'S GRACE,

SWEEPS ACROSS THE LAND

AND DRIVES THIS EVIL FROM MY LAND,

FAR FROM OUR DESERT SANDS.

PEOPLE OF THE NIGHT

I AM ALL THE PEOPLE OF THE NIGHT,

CAN'T YOU SEE,

I LIVE AMIDST THE DARKENED BUSH,

AND THE SHADOW OF THE TREE,

I'LL DRINK THE MILK OF CACTUS,

I'LL EAT THE DESERT SAND,

UNTIL A FLOOD OF RIGHTEOUSNESS

SWEEPS ACROSS THE LAND

AND DRIVES THIS EVIL WE WITHSTAND

FAR FROM OUR SACRED SANDS.

PEOPLE OF THE NIGHT

HARÉ BRAHMA!

YOU ARE MY ONLY COURSE,

HARÉ RAMA!

YOU ARE MY STRENGTH AND FORCE,

HARÉ SHIVA!

WON'T YOU DISPEL THIS CURSE SOMEHOW!

HARÉ VISHNU,

YOU ARE MY ONLY SOURCE,

HARÉ KRISHNA!

YOU ARE THE UNIVERSE,

HARÉ BRAHMA!

I NEED DIVINE RECOURSE RIGHT NOW!

NAOMAL

I AM ALL THE PEOPLE OF THE NIGHT

CAN'T YOU SEE,

I LIVE AMIDST THE DARKENED BUSH,

AND THE SHADOW OF THE TREE.

I'LL DRINK THE MILK OF SADNESS,

I'LL EAT THE BREAD OF PAIN,

UNTIL THE GOOD LORD SETS THINGS RIGHT,

THEN I'LL COME HOME AGAIN,

TO SEE MY WIFE AND CHILDREN DEAR,

CRY NO MORE IN VAIN.

PEOPLE OF THE NIGHT

HOME, HOME, HOME.

NAOMAL

OM, OM, OM.

PEOPLE OF THE NIGHT

WAR! WAR! WAR!

The lighting on Stage fades slowly.

OffStage the clang of clashing swords and booming cannons accompany loud commands of 'ready, aim, fire!' The sounds of a raging battle are intermingled with ejaculations of 'Allah hu Akbar' 'Bismillah' 'Jihad!' 'Islam is in danger!'

Women and Children wail as the chant "War, War, War" continues.

END OF ACT III

SCENE I

ACT III

SCENE 2

ACT III
SCENE 2

SETTING: *The private apartments of NUR MOHAMMED, Regent of Sindh at the Imperial Palace in Hyderabad, once King Murad Ali's bed chamber.*

On a table there is a single burning candle and The Holy Quran.

The sounds of battling armies continue from the previous scene.

The sounds become louder to suggest that the armed struggle is taking place in the vicinity of the Palace.

BEGUM MUMTAZ is silently muttering her prayers. NUR MOHAMMED stares vacantly.

Enter: An OFFICER of the Imperial Guard.

OFFICER
(Frantically)
Majesty, it is no longer safe to be here. The enemy is at the threshold. A raging fire consumes the south side. We must leave immediately while there is still time.

> *A volley of gunfire is heard. Reflections of light suggest that fire has broken out closer to the royal bedroom.*

OFFICER
We must leave now, Sire!

A SOLDIER
(OffStage)

Ya Allaha! The enemy has stormed the palace gates. The Palace is aflame, the war is lost, the war is lost!

NUR MOHAMMED

Leave Us! We desire to be alone.

OFFICER

Majesty, surely you see the danger to yourself and the Queen.

NUR MOHAMMED

Leave us! Go! Now!

> *The Officer salutes and exits.*

> *OffStage the sounds of general panic, cannon fire and exploding dynamite continue as NUR MOHAMMED draws his sword.*

> *He positions the blade point close to his chest. He leans forward on it. He dies silently. BEGUM MUMTAZ's eyes are closed as she moves her lips in silent meditation.*

> *Two COURTIERS enter the room and discover NUR MOHAMMED dead.*

COURTIER

The King is dead. Take whatever you can and run, save yourselves.

> *More SERVANTS and COURTIERS enter. Some place MUMTAZ on the floor and attempt to move the bed.*

COURTIER

Everyone knows that the Talpur kings slept with their treasures.

SECOND COURTIER
I hope they weren't referring to the whores they slept with.

Two COURTIERS look curiously at NUR MOHAMMED.

COURTIER
May you rot in hell!

The other COURTIER attempts to pry the rings off NUR MOHAMMED's dead fingers.

SECOND COURTIER
(To Nur Mohammed)
May Allah grant you seventy-two lizards for wives.

A hooded BABAJI enters. He heads directly to BEGUM MUMTAZ as she continues to mutter her prayers.

COURTIER
Who are you?

BABAJI
I am the keeper of the Sacred Crocodiles of Muggerpir. Help me get her out of here. I need her to feed the crocodiles.

COURTIER
Good! Feed the royal bitch to the crocodiles.

SECOND COURTIER
Yes, feed her to the crocodiles.

They help carry BEGUM MUMTAZ offstage as BRITISH SOLDIERS storm the room. The COURTIERS promptly surrender.

COURTIER

Thank Allah for his mercies. Long live Seth Naomal and the English for saving the kingdom.

BRITISH OFFICER

This Palace and the Capital are now under the control of British forces under the command of General Sir Charles Napier.

A British soldier carrying the Union Jack, and the Colors of the British East India Company enters, amidst general jubilation, and chants of victory: 'God save the Queen,' 'Long live General Charles Napier,' 'Hail to the freedom fighters,' 'Long live Seth Naomal', to the accompaniment of bagpipes.

END OF ACT III

SCENE 2

ACT III

SCENE 3

ACT III
SCENE 3

SETTING: *The Durbar Hall in the Palace at Hyderabad. The footstool, the spittoon, the table with the wine decanter and the partition have been removed. Upon the silver throne rests a portrait of Queen Victoria. The Union Jack and the flag of the British East India Company are planted on either side of the throne. The sounds of the bagpipes continue from the previous scene. BRITISH OFFICERS mingle with the GUESTS who represent the diversity of India. Among them are Parsis, Muslims, Sikhs, Hindus, Baluchis, Afghans dressed in their native costumes. English LADIES wearing elegant gowns are conspicuous by their presence. They stand in a group apart from the men. NAOMAL and POTTINGER exchange inaudible pleasantries with fellow invitees.*

POTTINGER
Naomal, Sorry to hear Seth Hotchand couldn't make it this evening.

NAOMAL
His self-imposed exile has taken its toll on his health. I do hope though that General Napier, our new Governor does not misconstrue his absence from his first official Durbar.

POTTINGER
Nonsense, Naomal. You are here and we all understand that your father would have been here too if his health permitted. There is something I have been wanting to say to you, dear friend. The talk in official circles in India and abroad credit the Battle of Miani as the single event that led to our victory in

116

Sindh. We who were in Sindh throughout the campaign know otherwise. Couldn't have done it without you and your people. This is your evening as much as anybody else's.

POTTINGER looks around the room noticing the guests.

POTTINGER
(Continuing)
Who are all these people!

NAOMAL
Landowners, merchants, civil servants, former horse thieves who stole your camels and horses a month earlier and sold them back to you yesterday. Come Henry, let me introduce you to a few.

Trumpets peel and cymbals clash as English soldiers escort His Excellency, GENERAL CHARLES NAPIER, a lean, intense, imposing man with a scraggly beard.

His military uniform is covered with medals. He stands behind the throne.

He is flanked by his AIDE DE CAMP and his SECRETARY, an Englishman in a severe black suit.

ENGLISH SOLDIER
His Excellency, the Governor of Sindh, General Sir Charles Napier!

NAPIER waves as the GUESTS give him a round of applause.

NAPIER notices HENRY POTTINGER and SETH NAOMAL

NAPIER
(To his Aide)
Who is that Blackyman with Henry?

AIDE
Sir, He is the famous Seth Naomal.

NAPIER
I see.

NAPIER approaches SETH NAOMAL and HENRY POTTINGER

NAOMAL respectfully bows at the waist to NAPIER

NAPIER
(Curtly to Seth Naomal)
Wherever I turn my steps in Sindh, I hear people proclaim your name and exclaim, Naomal! Naomal! I conquered Sindh by the power of my sword. What weapon did you wield, what did you ever do that the people should attribute the success of British arms to you?

He is quickly surrounded by GUESTS.

NAPIER exits with his AIDE DE CAMP and his SECRETARY,

Bearers in white uniforms and red turbans serve beverages to the guests.

The music gradually changes to the melody of the Sindh National Anthem played by the bagpipes.

The COURT JESTER bursts upon the stage wearing a black top hat, riding boots and a Victorian evening gown.

He has garish makeup and an exaggerated bosom.

He carries a whisky bottle in one hand and a cricket bat in the other.

The COURT JESTER tries to waltz with an ATTENDANT.

The GUESTS are amused as the ATTENDANT shrugs him off.

The COURT JESTER chases him around the stage.

The GUESTS applaud.

He continues his antics, interacting with the guests, pretending to drink from the bottle. He bursts into song, as the melody of the Sindh Anthem begins.

JESTER

DISPENSERS OF JUSTICE,

DECIDERS OF THINGS,

OH, GIVERS OF CIVILIZATION,

DISPOSERS OF SULTANS AND NABOBS AND KINGS,

IT'S TIME FOR ALL ROUND CELEBRATION.

THE BRITISH ARE HERE,

THE BRITISH ARE HERE,

THE TALPURS ARE GONE,

THERE'S NOTHING TO FEAR,

SO, BOTTOMS UP THE WHISKY,

LET'S GUZZLE SOME BEER,

THE BRITISH ARE HERE,

THE BRITISH ARE HERE.

SUNG BY ALL

BETWEEN THE MOUNTAINS AND THE PLAINS OF HIND,

LIE THE GOLDEN SANDS OF BELOVED SINDH,

ALL SINDHIS HAIL IN A SINGLE VOICE,

GENERAL NAPIER IS ALLAH'S CHOICE!

SETH NAOMAL IS BRAHMA'S CHOICE!

A HINDU

HE IS BRAHMA'S CHOICE!

A MUSLIM

HE IS ALLAH'S CHOICE!

HINDUS

BRAHMAS CHOICE! BRAHMA'S CHOICE!

MUSLIMS

ALLAH'S CHOICE! ALLAH'S CHOICE!

Sung to the melody of the battle hymn

ALLAH!

HINDUS

BRAHMA!

The Allah/Brahma exchange continues. Low voices offstage sing along.

VOICES

(Offstage)

LORD OF LORDS, KING OF KINGS, GOD OF GODS.

The music reverts to the Sindh National Anthem again. The JESTER meanders among the guests as he pretends to play an imaginary game of Cricket.

JESTER

DISPENSERS OF JUSTICE,

DECIDERS OF THINGS,

OH, GIVERS OF CIVILIZATION,

DISPOSERS OF SULTANS AND NABOBS AND KINGS,

IT'S TIME FOR ALL ROUND CELEBRATION.

THE BRITISH ARE HERE,

THE BRITISH ARE HERE,

NUR MOHAMMED IS DEAD,

AND THERE'S NOTHING TO FEAR,

SO, LETS GUZZLE SOME WHISKY,

LET'S CHUGLUG SOME BEER,

THE BRITISH ARE HERE,

THE BRITISH ARE HERE.

BETWEEN THE MOUNTAINS AND THE PLAINS OF HIND,

LIE THE GOLDEN SANDS OF BELOVED SINDH,

ALL SINDHIS HAIL IN A SINGLE VOICE,

AREY BLOODY CRICKET IS ALLAH'S CHOICE,

> *There is loud cheering from the guests as the JESTER continues to play an imaginary game of cricket.*

HINDUS

BLOODY CRICKET IS BRAHMA'S CHOICE.

MUSLIMS

BLOODY CRICKET IS ALLAH'S CHOICE.

HINDUS

IT'S BRAHMA'S CHOICE!

> *The music and the singing get more passionate. The dancing, singing, and the revelry continue as the lighting on stage gets dimmer. Silhouettes and shadows dance as the stage is plunged in darkness.*

> *A spot focuses on a silhouette that is revealed as a dancing CROCODILE. A second spot picks up another dancing CROCODILE as the music reaches a crescendo. A Strobe light reveals several CROCODILES dancing. The music drowns out the voices. The CROCODILES exit the stage one after the other. Each exit is accompanied by the sound of a splash. The music gets softer and gives way gradually*

to the sounds of chirping birds accompanied by a flute playing the serene melody of the song, "The Child in Me is Crying," sung by BEGUM MUMTAZ in an earlier scene.

The stage is bathed in dawn's early light. The glow of a swinging lantern adds an orange tint to the bluish green light. NAOMAL enters with ALU and BABAJI.

ALU

Grandpa, is it day already? I had the most beautiful dream. I saw crocodiles dancing. I saw you. I saw your father. There were forests and Englishmen, palaces, battles, and a beautiful princess.

BEGUM MUMTAZ enters as the melody of 'The Child in Me is Crying' plays softly. She wears a white gown and is slightly stooped with age. She walks in a daze She stares lovingly at ALU. She approaches him. She touches his face, and plays with his hair. She has tears running down her face.

MUMTAZ
(To Babaji)

The Prince you promised me!

MUMTAZ smiles, chuckles. She holds back tears, and laughs hysterically.

ALU slowly backs away from her towards NAOMAL.

A moment of silence.

BABAJI

Come Highness, we must prepare the place. In a few hours visitors from near and far will be here to feed the crocodiles.

MUMTAZ stares at SETH NAOMAL.

MUMTAZ

(*In a voice as crisp, clear and authoritative as the young, imperious Princess Begum Mumtaz.*)

Seth Naomal have you fully avenged the wrongs inflicted upon your father? Do you now feel satisfied?

She laughs hysterically.

SETH NAOMAL stops in mid-stride.

He turns to face MUMTAZ and BABAJI. He bows to both. He reaches for ALU'S hand.

The Sufi Singer, Fateh Ali Khan's rendition of Dum Dum Mast Qalandar begins to play.

BABAJI raises his right hand skyward and begins the Sama, (The Dance of the Whirling Dervishes) called the Dhamaal in Sindh.

As the song continues, BABAJI starts to spin and whirl.

BEGUM MUMTAZ raises her hand skyward and starts to spin and whirl.

NAOMAL raises his right hand skyward.

He starts to spin and whirl.

ALU raises his right hand skyward.

He starts to spin and whirl.

All four on stage spin and whirl faster

and faster.

Multi colored strobe lights bathe the stage.

The four dance themselves into a trance.

CURTAIN

THE END